Theological Education
for Social Ministry

Contributors

Terence R. Anderson is Professor of Christian Ethics, Vancouver School of Theology, British Columbia.

James D. Beumler is a Presbyterian minister and doctoral candidate in American Religious History, Princeton University, New Jersey.

Jacquelyn Grant is Assistant Professor of Systematic Theology, Interdenominational Theological Center, Atlanta, Georgia.

Dieter T. Hessel completed this book when he was Associate for Social Education, the Program Agency, Presbyterian Church (USA), New York City. He is now Director, PCUSA Committee on Social Witness Policy, Louisville, Kentucky.

Karen Lebacqz is Professor of Christian Ethics, Pacific School of Religion, Berkeley, California.

James C. Logan is Professor of Systematic Theology, Wesley Theological Seminary, Washington, D.C.

Larry L. Rasmussen is Reinhold Niebuhr Professor of Social Ethics, Union Theological Seminary, New York City.

Ronald H. Stone is Professor of Social Ethics, Pittsburgh Theological Seminary, Pennsylvania.

Theological Education for Social Ministry

Edited by
Dieter T. Hessel

The Pilgrim Press
New York

The biblical quotations in this book are from the *Revised Standard Version of the Bible,*
copyright 1946, 1955, and © 1971, 1973 by the Division of Christian Education,
National Council of Churches, and are used by permission.

Library of Congress Cataloging-in-Publication Data

Theological education for social ministry / edited by Dieter T. Hessel.
  Bibliography: p. 172.

  ISBN 0-8298-0773-X (pbk.)

  1. Theology—Study and teaching—United States—Congresses.
2. Church and social problems—United States—Congresses.
I. Hessel, Dieter T.

BV4030.T49 1988

207'.73—dc19   87-32700

The Pilgrim Press, 132 West 31 Street, New York, NY 10001

To the teachers of theology who encouraged and equipped us for a ministry of justice and peace

Contents

Preface

The papers in this collection were commissioned for and discussed at a Washington, D.C., Symposium on Theological Education for Socially Responsible Ministry, January 8–10, 1987. This event was developed by the Social Education staff of the Presbyterian Program Agency and was supported financially by the Lilly Endowment, Religion Division. The gathering was chaired by three Wesley Theological Seminary faculty members—an ethicist, a biblical scholar, and a systematic theologian—and was attended by an ecumenical mix of twenty other participants: teachers of ethics, theology, church and society, and religious education, and several people who work as pastors or denominational staff, who were sent to the symposium by an educational agency of their communion.

Symposium participants represented Lutheran, United Methodist, Presbyterian, United Church of Christ, Disciples of Christ, and Episcopal traditions, and they came from almost every region of the United States and from British Columbia. The presence and participation of pastors served as a healthy reminder of the connection between theological education and the practice of parish ministry.

We wrote, discussed, and now share these papers in order to help communities of theological study "go public," i.e., to cohere around the task of preparing for faithful, effective public ministry. Specific purposes of the project launched with this symposium are to:

1. comprehend a dynamic, whole conception of social ministry and its necessary accents through the next decade;
2. clarify what seminarians most need to learn to equip them for faithful, effective leadership in public life;
3. explore the subject matter and methods of curricula that orient and enliven the social witness and ministry of pastors working with their congregations and communties; and
4. specify how a basic cycle of theological study, as well as related programs of higher education and continuing education, can teach the necessary content and skills.

Dieter T. Hessel

1

A Social Agenda for Theological Study

Dieter T. Hessel

The times have turned, and progressive social ferment is evident again. Conservative reaction has run its course. A new cycle of societal change exposes public readiness for affirmative government and policy reform.[1] Ours is a pivotal cultural occasion in which movements of liberating faith intersect with yearnings for economic justice, ecological care, community health, and demilitarized foreign policy.

But how ready and willing are the churches locally, regionally, and nationally to move beyond self-protective habits into proactive witness and ministry? In these fermenting times what will parish leaders contribute to prophetic critique and social invention? How shall the seminaries prepare ministers to make a public difference?

The chapters in this book reflect an informal consensus about the public ministry to be engendered in theological education. Together they affirm the importance and specify

1

basic dynamics of socially responsible ministry. But they make no attempt to arrive at a simple definition, since social ministry involves the whole life of the church.

One symposium author and participant, Karen Lebacqz, drew out of her rereading of our papers these rich elements of a composite definition.

- *Socially responsible ministry* (SRM) involves a "radical critique" of society, depending in part on careful listening to the oppressed. It is lived Christian practice that "envisions the whole," placing ministry in the context of large social trends. (Rasmussen)
- There is no neutral ministry. All ministry is socially responsive in some way; the question is how. SRM is a liberating ministry that emerges concretely out of the (black) oppressed community. (Grant)
- SRM requires social analysis and consciousness of the ethos in which we live. It demands personal, institutional, and ecclesial self-critique. It is not the same as a focus on social issues. (Stone)
- SRM features praxis or struggle for liberation of the oppressed. It requires critical awareness of tendencies that derive from our own social location. SRM needs memory and vision—past and future. (Lebacqz)
- SRM follows the logic of *missio dei* in its wholeness, and participates in the unified mission of the church. It develops as Christians become story-formed, worshiping-and-witnessing people who have theological discipline and are socioculturally aware. (Logan)
- SRM is oriented to doing justice, making peace, and caring for creation. It requires walking with the oppressed in shared ministry and in working for social policy change. It affirms the communal nature of human existence and is expressed in all the basic functions of the church. (Hessel)
- SRM requires "solidarity"—loyalty to disregarded people, not ideological causes. It is rooted in spirituality and love, guided by the vision of shalom. It requires critical analysis and institutional reform. (Anderson)

2

The symposium papers delineate a mission framework for seminary education, and they propose new departures—both demanding and practical—for theological study to engender socially responsible ministry. Each paper also specifies what people who are preparing for ministerial leadership ought to be taught and how to learn it. Reform of curriculum and pedagogy is nothing new to theological academies (in some schools curriculum revision is a chronic condition). But most recent reforms have done relatively little to integrate preparation for social ministry into basic courses of study for pastoral leadership. This problem in theological (and parish) education deserves careful attention by all who would undergird the church's mission in society.

A Common Need

Organizing the symposium, commissioning and editing its papers, and then holding conversations on location at several seminaries helped me to discern major developments and difficulties in the efforts of mainline denominational and interdenominational theological schools to educate for social ministry. Here is an initial overview of their common situation and need as I see it.

1. Seminaries that serve the progressive denominations are generally concerned to educate a new, maturer constituency for contemporary social responsibility. This concern reflects their changing composition, growing ecumenical awareness, and alertness to current issues but shows little intentional planning to educate seminary students for social ministry. Student bodies and faculties, from the 1970s forward, have included more minority people and many more women. The Association of Theological Schools in the United States and Canada reported that in 1972, only 10.2 percent of seminary students were women; by 1984, 25 percent were women. Black enrollment doubled from 2.6 percent to 5.2 percent. Today, in some theological schools, the ratio of women to men students is about equal. Meanwhile the average age of students has gone up, and nearly one

3

third are part-time, often employed, changing career. The changing composition of the seminary community has re-shaped social consciousness, particularly through teaching and study of liberation theologies—black, Latin American, Asian, and feminist. Each of these theological movements raises systemic questions about faithful life and witness, and would liberate North American theological education from its white, male, middle-class, and monocultural limitations.

2. Global ecumenical awareness has become prominent in North American theological education. Seminary attention to global education and cross-cultural learning was prompted by the maturation of the ecumenical church toward more mutuality in mission, leading some autonomous churches in the Two-Thirds world to send missionaries to North American Christians (although not as much as the other way around).

The quest for global solidarity is the primary way that theological education challenged the new 1980s conservatism marked by parochial values, ecumenical indifference, socio-economic complacency, privatizing religiousness, and professional careerism. Jose Miguez-Bonino said in 1981 to the U.S./Canadian Consultation on Global Solidarity in Theological Education held in Toronto:

> Global solidarity is necessary in order to know God, not only to be able to express our solidarity with somebody else!
>
> We need to ask how is global solidarity present every-where in the theological program. . . . The battle for global solidarity in theological education is fought and won or lost in the teaching of the Bible, Church History, Systematic The-ology, Pastoral Theology.[2]

The Toronto consultation, sponsored by the World Council of Churches, was a serious effort to prepare guidelines, strat-egies, and structures for the theological curricula that deal seriously with both global realities and local contexts. It emphasized that three types of things—reflective experi-ences, resources of knowledge, and social relations—are nec-essary to work in global solidarity. Yet, despite presentations by J. Deotis Roberts and Lawrence Jones calling for urban

4

consciousness, the 1981 gathering on global justice, paid scant attention to the parish struggle for geographic ecumenicity in cities and counties.

In the intervening years seminaries have failed to fill the void left by the demise of urban (or rural) community organization and action training. The irony of that failure is that these same seminaries profess greater commitment to prepare students for local church ministry than did many seminaries two decades ago.

3. The basic three-year (M.Div.) cycle of theological study generally is not preparing ministers to meet the evident public needs of the near social future. I have already mentioned the lack of attention to equipping leaders for urgent community rebuilding tasks in the 1990s.

Another requirement for meeting the near future is to comprehend, and respond with prophetic integrity to, basic cultural dynamics, ideological biases, and competing interests that shape the secular ethos of ministry. These concerns of any faithful community are the focus of the first few chapters of this book. They highlight the importance of engaging public reality by doing incisive social analysis, teaching a coherent social philosophy, and participating in transforming action.

These requirements point in a direction that contrasts sharply with the prevailing pattern of clergy training. It seems that many seminaries have acquiesced to a reductionist or circumscribed model of pastoral ministry, limiting it to an "insulated church box." Not that everyone fell into that pattern, but too many equippers and evaluators of parish pastors have accepted the notion that local church ministry is with and for existing members of the congregation. As if Jesus never stressed the larger communal purpose "that they may have life . . . abundantly," or a shepherding role with "other sheep, that are not of this fold" (John 10:15). Pastors and other parish leaders are in real danger of becoming mere chaplains to, or managers of, timid congregations, instead of developing the church's public connections, presence, and service. Seminaries can help students break out of the box by emphasizing course work that prepares pastors,

5

local church officers, and committed laity for lively parish leadership and whole public ministry in a time of greater social opportunity and danger.

4. Currently, when social ministry focus does occur in basic courses, it is more likely to give general attention to theological foundations for social involvement than to explore the contemporary dynamics of social witness and ministry. This observation is based on my conversations with experienced seminary professors and on the results of a seminary survey done by the Presbyterian Advisory Council on Church and Society. It asked denominationally related seminaries how they "prepare the ministerial leadership that will sustain and guide the social witness of the church." As the survey suggested,

> that process involves theological and biblical exposition, social analysis in a consistent ethical framework, interpretation and education, and the development of policies, strategies and programs of social witness. The preparation undertaken by the theological school should result in:
>
> - understanding of and commitment to the biblical and theological tradition that undergirds the Reformed approach to vocation and witness in the public life of the society, through individual Christians and as a corporate body;
> - knowledge of the social teaching, social policy, and major social program directions adopted by General Assembly;
> - skill in the effective communication, interpretation, and implementation of the church's social witness.

The seminary survey results reported to the 1985 PCUSA General Assembly show that only the first of these three components is found often in class discussion and student papers. In student life there is more opportunity, although rather scattered or "invisible," for involvement in justice and peace action or reflection. Little of this activity has longevity.

5. Learning to engage issues of justice and peace happens informally in seminary community events and groups much more often than it does in regular course work. This extracurricular pattern of education in community usually involves topical mealtime discussions (e.g., "ethics luncheons"), occa-

sional guest speakers, or short-term, project-oriented task forces. A few seminaries also offer annual communitywide miniseminars on one or more social dynamics (e.g., racism, militarism, sexism, ageism, naturism).

Such events or group activities can be quite clarifying and motivating. But what kind of discipline and competence does informal, extracurricular learning develop among its participants? It should be noted that important learning by example, both positive and negative, occurs this way. Positively, an engaged seminary group can engender commitment to social ministry. Negatively, it may reinforce the image of social witness as episodic or optional, rather than teach a basic social approach to parish ministry. Here we see a classic example of being taught style and strategy (willy-nilly) by what the community does.

Education for social ministry involves action/reflection and touches the whole system. Seminaries that discern this reality will focus more on socially responsible ways of ministering than on fragmented issue analysis/action.

6. Seminaries still tend to approach education for social ministry in limited or optional rather than in systemic ways. A wholistic vision of ministry is not usually shared by specialized faculty, and only the rare theological academy seeks such consensus.

Professors in the classical disciplines who do focus on social ministry are unusual. Teachers in the theological academy remain uneasy with a wholistic public ministry focus that bridges the specialized academic disciplines that their careers feature. They prefer instead to relegate the subject of social ministry to elective courses in Christianity and Society attached to the Practical Department, and to available field work opportunities where seasoned professionals—parish practitioners and other creative ministers—have, at best, secondary teaching roles.

Still there are some important innovations in group study across fields of Bible, history, theology-ethics. A few faculties are now meeting together to explore basic topics of contemporary theological concern in quest of a common framework (not merely to brief each other on their study projects). Experimental faculty-student groups are also forming to study major subjects of theological-ethical emphasis that cut across fields (e.g., feminist, black, or other liberation theology).

Meanwhile practical theology itself is the subject of some quality rethinking. Joseph Hough and John Cobb have proposed two current images of those who minister as professional church leaders: (1) Practical Christian Thinker, who is a pathfinder, and (2) Reflective Practitioner in leadership style. They combine these two images into one portrait of the minister as Practical Theologian.[3]

Ecclesial praxis—that is, "critical and constructive reflection on and guidance for the praxis of the community"—is the organizing center of practical theology, in the view of James Fowler.[4] Although his prime interest is Christian formation, Fowler also values education for personal and social transformation guided by the normative sources and vision of Christian faith. Fowler's practical theology overview encourages restlessness with the standard academic model of theological "encyclopaedia."

Charles Wood takes us another step by challenging the dominant theory-to-practice model of theological study. He asserts that wherever the validity of this model is assumed,

> historical and philosophical theology then make no use of the resources which practical theology has to offer to their own tasks. The scope of their inquiries becomes artificially restricted in ways which lead to distorted understanding, and which make it difficult, in turn, for practical theology to appropriate their resources for its own inquiry.[5]

Wood urges seminaries to develop critical habits and to strengthen the

> practical dimension of theological reflection upon doctrine.
>
> Theologians as a rule have been much more adept at analyzing, criticizing, and reforming doctrines than at reflecting critically upon the actual performance of witness. . . . Theology has typically been concerned with the *content*, to the neglect of the *function*, of doctrine. If so, the solution is not to shift focus from doctrine to some other area, but rather to

broaden the focus so as to bring into view the way doctrine actually serves (or fails to serve, or might better serve) as an instrument for the regulation of the church's existence.[6]

A reverse process of theological reflection on praxis would complete the circle.

7. Theological educators show increasing concern to elicit the commitment and to nurture competencies that are crucial for leadership in social ministry. There has been a seminary resurgence of community worship and spiritual formation disciplines, some of which foster contemplation of and prayer for the suffering world. This development signals a concern to ground doing and thinking in authentic being.

There is also some institutional movement toward intentional competency-based education for public ministry (see chapter 9). For example, Vancouver Theological Seminary, British Columbia, seeks to develop social ministry competencies as part of its educational mission, and to evaluate these competencies in faculty and peer review of the students' "exit knowledge." (As graduation approaches, Vancouver conducts a week-long event concerned with integration of knowledge. Its content is somewhat comparable to denominational ordination examinations in using case studies, but the style is communal.)

Although the familiar course model of education puts the priority on getting credits and mastering subject matter, a competency model invites a wholistic focus on knowledge, skills, and personal spiritual development. Learning becomes an interdisciplinary process with varied pedagogy and content at M.Div. and continuing education levels. In this model, faculty are teachers of, and classes offer group resources for learning, competencies. Each "department" is responsible for helping the whole institution foster an appropriate cluster of competencies. The goal for learners is to acquire and use integrated knowledge in Christian ministry.

What kind of competencies are to be learned? Various seminaries offer plural answers. As is suggested in the later chapters of this book, leaders of ministry in society need

9

enough knowledge and skill to analyze a changing society and their own lives in theological-ethical perspective; to focus this analysis on public issues in their local/regional setting; to minister in solidarity with vulnerable people; to clarify strategic, flexible ways for the church to meet community needs; and to foster larger public responsibility. My own symposium paper, chapter 7, identifies ten habits and related abilities of leaders of congregations that are justice-active.

8. In educating parish leaders, seminaries have a promising opportunity to utilize liberating pedagogy that takes praxis and social location seriously (see chapters 3, 4, and 5) and that intentionally seeks to overcome the mind-sets that block socially responsible ministry (see chapter 8). Theological educators are increasingly interested in teaching methods and ways of learning that motivate as well as equip ministers to develop the church's faithful, effective public involvement.

The experience to share and know how to acquire in order to lead a whole strategy of social ministry encompasses five interactive dimensions of a nonsequential spiral that the learner can enter at any point.

a. *Theological reflection*—exploring theological visions in scripture and tradition, in dialogue with contemporary experience, and exercising a confessing, hermeneutical imagination in this context.

b. *Social analysis*—analyzing realities of our personal-public-institutional situation by consulting various sources, by moving through a process of hearing and telling stories, and by doing homework that utilizes behavioral sciences, literature, and the arts.

c. *Mission engagement*—participating reflectively in a social praxis through multiple modes of ministry focused on priority concerns of the church.

d. *Social ethics*—clarifying ethical norms that have theological warrant and are contextually pertinent, and helping the church become a community of moral dialogue that faces ethical dilemmas and articulates key values for social policy/personal practice.

10

e. *Social action*—taking up specific opportunities for, and utilizing particular methods of, social service-reform-resistance to meet public issues.

Curriculum Analysis

The symposium on theological education for social ministry also reviewed a prepared analysis of curriculum emphases over the past fifteen years that are detectable in the catalogues of institutions at which authors of the commissioned papers currently teach. Chapter 9 of this book presents a revised version of that seminary curriculum analysis—expanded to encompass ten seminaries of various Protestant communions and supplemented by conversation with faculty and students in those schools.

Two reasons for this rather unrepresentative seminary curriculum sample were first, to take some pressure off the authors of symposium papers, allowing them to concentrate more on presenting fresh concepts than on reviewing what is (or isn't) being done in their school's curriculum; and second, to provide symposium participants and readers of these papers with a brief overview of curriculum trends in theological education that affect preparation for social ministry.

The criteria we used in the curriculum analysis are drawn from a striking model entitled "A Theological Curriculum for the 1970's," published in *Theological Education* Magazine (1968), as well as from two recent books, Edward Farley, *Theologia* (Fortress Press, 1983), and Theodore W. Jennings Jr., ed., *The Vocation of the Theologian* (Fortress Press, 1985).

Although only a limited number of seminary curricula were examined in this study, it was a useful way to clarify some important curriculum- and community-assessment questions. We encourage seminary students, teachers, and administrators to ask similar questions about what is being learned to undergird socially responsible ministry in their school. We also assume that congregations and church agencies will want to ask parallel questions.

Learning Again to Be the Church in the World

A vital community of faith—whether congregation or seminary—which would develop laity and clergy alike to make a public difference, is bound to ask questions similar to those being explored here. In fact, as can be seen in the nearly forgotten literature on theological education, many of our social ministry concerns are not new to theological education. Thus a book of papers on *The Making of Ministers,* published a quarter century ago, emphasizes the need to educate leaders for servanthood in the world—to become "equipped for every good work" (2 Timothy). What theological students must learn is outlined there in terms of articulate faith, disciplined skills, and suasive power to lead the church as a voluntary community of faith active in the "energy fields" of society. And Arnold Nash, proposing what we now call a whole approach to theological study that cuts across separate fields, reminds us:

> Religion is so ubiquitous and so significant in human affairs that we mislead ourselves in thought if we regard theology as one field among others, just as we misinterpret it in life if we view religion as one interest among others; and hence, particularly in a fragmented world like that of the twentieth century, we should put our stress on religion as that which holds things together, rather than as a substantive field of study.[7]

In 1964 we also find Reuel Howe vigorously criticizing a "parochial" image of ministry that contradicts the lively doctrine of the church developing in ecumenical circles.

> Both clergy and laity think of the church in terms of the local congregation and its internal concerns. . . . The relation to the world of politics, law, and custom is either not thought of at all or done ambiguously. Neither is there awareness among many people of the meanings being expressed by the plastic and performing arts, by science and industry, and the significance they have for the meanings of the Gospel. The parochialism of this image of the church often reduces Christian faith and practice to the dimensions of a cult.[8]

A quarter of a century later much has changed but little has changed. Theological education remains in chronic conflict over its centering focus. Now, in the setting of North American society entering the last decade of the twentieth century, the study of theology must be reformed again to develop leadership that nurtures socially responsible faith and that leads the believing community into effective engagement.

2

The Near Future of Socially Responsible Ministry

Perspectives from Christian Ethics

Larry L. Rasmussen

Everybody's Doing It

The subject of Christian ethics is the moral life. Christian ethics thus addresses the kinds of people, communities, societies, indeed the kind of world we are to be, as well as the relationships, institutions, and actions becoming of that.

Just as every organization of knowledge is invariably a point of view, so also education of most any kind is always *an exercise in moral formation.* Seminary education may be more aware of moral formation than some other kinds of education, since the sponsoring communities (the church and the university) are either theological-moral in their very identity (the church) or committed to moral inquiry and discourse (the university). But no education fails to address the moral life in some manner. Everybody does it, even when few admit it.

14

Consider the seminary curriculum. One might study languages, gain musical knowledge, or learn to write verbatims for Clinical Pastoral Education, all without *directly* addressing morality. But the minute these learned skills are used—exegesis for a sermon, music for the worship service, counseling for the discouraged—the Christian moral life is joined, for better or worse. There simply isn't a way to study or teach scripture, church history, systematic theology, communications and the arts, or any of the tools necessary to the practice of ministry without subtly shaping our moral "being" and "doing." If we add to classroom experiences the further experiences of campus worship and other public moments together, such as conversations in refectory, hallway, and living quarters, or if we join in action together around some project or cause, then it is clear that no one in a seminary fails to influence and color the Christian moral life. Those who are professionally trained teachers of Christian Ethics are only a tiny minority of the effective "teachers" of ethics and morality.

To recognize that "everybody's doing it" is already to recognize something about "socially responsible ministry." It is to recognize, for example, that the phrase itself is redundant in at least one sense. We are, from birth, social beings. Granted, our society fosters the grand illusion that the self is prior to, or independent of, social influence and formation. We like to think there is some core in our lives that is not subject to our "social" self. Yet we cannot even *think* this without language. And language already encodes and communicates social meanings. That is much of its purpose.

Differently said, there is no ministry that is not, at every point, "social" in character. If human beings are involved, ministry is irreducibly "social." We are social beings.

To understand ministry as inherently social, however, is not yet to judge it "responsible." That entails moral judgments; and these are usually made in the subtlest ways by "everyone." That is, they occur as a matter of social ethos and process; as an expression of cultural assumptions and learning; as an outcome of seminary and church socialization. This means that some version of "socially responsible ministry" is always present, as a factual reality. But precisely what defines "responsibility" is very often both assumed and unexamined. It is present as a matter of ethos and enculturation and is institutionalized in myriad "social" ways. It is often only half-formed and half-articulated.

One of the tasks of Christian ethics is to render these nearly invisible assumptions and this formation visible. It is to expose the notion of "responsibility" present in ministry and make assessment of it. We must hold the notion of "responsibility" itself accountable, for ministry is always social in character and always "responsive" to some group or groups and to some understanding of the world and our task in it. What are these? becomes one of the questions put by Christian ethics to ministry.

Accents of the Late Twentieth Century

Let us, for purposes of discussion, grant that everyone in seminary education does effect some dimension of the Christian moral life. Let us also assume that ministry is always "socially responsible" in a descriptive sense, if not yet a normative one. And let us assume that our view of the world and our task in it are important to any definition of "socially responsible ministry." Can we go on to say something about the world, now, in which the Christian life is lived? Can we describe into view some of the social substance that ministry today should confront?

Of itself, such a profile does not answer the *normative* question of what socially responsible ministry ought to be, now. But no answer to that question can be given *apart* from such a sketch. If our view of things is not made explicit, it will simply be assumed, and acted on, without examination. What follows, then, is meant as a foil of sorts. It is a way by which we can discuss what socially responsible ministry might be today. The discussion is stimulated by the work of Ernst Troeltsch.

In *The Social Teachings of the Christian Churches* Troeltsch's burning question was the viability of Christian faith in the

16

modern world. For Troeltsch, "modern" referred to the first quarter of this century, stretching from there back to the Enlightenment, and chiefly in Europe. But his modern world is still recognizable: a world of industrialization and urbanization, secularism, pluralism, historical and cultural relativism, heightened human autonomy, increased individualism, capitalism, and socialism as driving forces, and a shrinking world under the enormous impact of science and technology everywhere.

As Troeltsch pursued his inquiry about Christianity's viability he discovered that the answer turned "on matters of ethics." So his question became, in considerable measure, a question of the viability of Christian ethics. Since for Troeltsch, Christian ethics was a virtual synonym for *lived Christian practice*, the question was finally the viability of the practiced Christian life for addressing the great issues of the day. These were social issues and an attendant inner and outer "coherence" for civilization, or, more precisely for Troeltsch, the *absence* of such coherence in modern society.

It was, then, Troeltsch's worry about viable Christian faith amid modernity that sent him on his grand search of the church's social teachings and social formation, to see what elements of a usable past were there. His conclusions are too numerous for consideration here, but two must be mentioned.

1. At the major turning points in history, "ethics" becomes a chief concern. It becomes the place where the past is tested as viable, or not viable, for the coming era. What ought we now to be and do, in the face of deep change and new chances? What configurations of life together will probably enhance good and restrain evil, rather than vice versa, given altered conditions and a new array of possibilities? What do we draw on to answer these questions?

Major turning times in history usually entail massive social experimentation. Some of it is chosen, most of it is the outcome of felt necessity, "choice" only within sharp constraints. New forms of Christian practice, and deep challenges to inherited practice, are part of this. "Ethics," as this experimentation in the lived Christian life, moves to the center of concern for both action *and* reflection in such times. In Karl Barth's sentence "Every revolution in dogmatics is preceded by a revolution in ethics." We are invariably caught up in social change, always responding in some way, sometimes initiating.

All this reiterates Troeltsch's discovery of the vital place of ethics in times of major social and intellectual change.

2. The second finding is closely related. But it requires so much elaboration that it must be given separate attention under two headings: emerging movements, and technology and power. The first draws directly on Troeltsch's findings. The second does not, yet it describes the character of the modern age that he insisted must be squarely faced if our ministry is to be socially viable and responsible.

Emerging movements. The great moments of religious renewal of the kind that launched a vibrant Christianity on the world happened with the *convergence* of two movements, movements usually separate from each other. One movement was that of dynamic *community-creating religion among lower socioeconomic classes.* Here an urgent sense of clear, stark human need was married to a simple faith full of feeling and energy. This was empowering religion facing matters of existential and material urgency. The other movement was that of the *conceptual revisioning of inherited faith traditions in a time of deep, and often bewildering, change.* Here cultivated criticism and speculative, constructive exploration occurred.

When these two came together—bold, sophisticated thought and community-creating religion at the base and edges of society—time turned a corner and new religious vitalities were loosed on the world. Many of them shook their world and at the same time gave it new direction.

But they had to join forces. Intellectual revisioning without the base communities didn't get farther uptown or downcountry than the addresses of scholars writing books at one another. And community-creating religious movements without bold thinkers who identified with them and came

18

from, or joined, their ranks didn't move outside their social backwaters and lagoons. The movements alone didn't become widespread, socially transforming forces. Potency required the active alliance,[1] as happened when that sect of messianic Judaism following Jesus found its Paul and John; or its Augustine in the weary, late days of the Empire; or its Luther amid the sixteenth-century's turmoil; or today in the theological-moral articulation of the liberating faith of Latin America and of South African base communities.

Ours is a moment fraught with this possibility. New community-creating religious faith joins bold thought among struggling sectors of the populace. These sectors might fall along socioeconomic class lines (the poor), along gender lines (women), along racial lines (the Black Church). In any event, discussion of "socially responsible ministry" should attend to the double dynamic here, or it is itself neither responsive nor responsible. The vitality of Christian faith in this age resides in the movements of struggling peoples. They are the teachers of first rank here. Socially responsible ministry is being forged here if it is being forged anywhere. We need to think long and hard about seminary curriculum, recruitment, and community in light of this.

Technology and power. Noting the locus of robust faith today is not the same as describing the distinctive mark of our age. To say what animates the church today is not to say what animates the seminaries' other partner, the university. And it certainly is not to say what the dominating powers of the wider world are. Third World and women's movements may, for example, hold the most *promise* for religiously empowered social transformation. They may even move to the center of socially responsible ministry. But that does not, of itself, describe what is empirically most forceful in the making of the modern epoch. Nor does it clarify what the existing prominent powers of our age mean for crafting responsible ministry.

A sketch of those dominant powers will hardly suffice. But it can begin a discussion.

A strong candidate for the special mark of our age is this

one: *the quantum leap in human knowledge and human power, the close correlation between this knowledge and this power, and the novel range, objects, and consequences of this knowledge and power.*

This may sound benign. It isn't, since the quantum leap is a leap in human *power,* not in human wisdom or moral maturity. Indeed ours is the most death-dealing century to date, with even greater promise silently waiting in the missile silos, and elsewhere.

How can the distinctive trait of the age be described? It might go something like this. The engine of capitalist and socialist industrial civilization alike is applied science (scientific knowing married to technological power). The "script" of applied science is nicely summarized in Hans Jonas' rendition of Francis Bacon's program: "Knowledge is aimed for power over nature and power over nature is aimed for improvement of the human lot."[2] Here we view ourselves over against the rest of nature—indeed over against the world—as subject working on object. The natural environment is "stuff" for human knowing, human design, human transformation. The world is the object of active human control for perceived human good.

There is a more compact way to say this. For the modern world, knowledge is power and power is control.

Bacon's object was the natural environment only. But the uses of science and "technique" are hardly limited to non-human nature. So we add Marx's name to what will become a quartet that stands in for a chorus of millions. Marx represents the turn to *society* as the object of powerful knowledge for human transformation. He helps to establish a *science of society* and makes of social analysis a tool for social change. Society becomes the object, and applied knowledge the power, for manipulation in the direction desired by the wielders of knowledge married to power.

If Marx places "society" on an agenda already listing "nature," Freud adds "psyche" or "self." The general approach is, in a most significant way, similar, but the object of knowing changes. That is, science "knows" in a subject/object outcome. Here, however, the self itself is both the knower and the known, the object of the subject. Consider the following advertisement from a bulletin board at the American University, Washington, D.C.:

> Interpersonal Skill-Building Groups: In these 10-session skill-focused groups, students will be taught to monitor and master anxiety . . . improve social skills by learning to be appropriately assertive.

The flier goes on to speak of "designing experiences" and acquiring techniques for "establishing trust." The goal is to teach the self "to monitor and master" its own "anxiety" by positioning itself rightly in a web of relationships of which it is part and that it can, with knowledge as power, help to "construct." The world of the psyche joins nature and society as worlds known and controlled by human power. The world is subject to engineering and management.

It would be wrong to claim that the knowledge/power/control complex is a uniquely modern one. That, of itself, is not the contention here, even though modernity has exuded a unique confidence in human power to effect desired human ends. The contention itself is that a *quantum leap in knowledge/power means a novel range of impact, novel objects, and novel consequences.*[3]

The end points on the life spectrum—life's beginning and life's ending—will illustrate. Fifty years ago we did not possess the capacity to terminate life as we know it on this particular patch of cosmic real estate. It is certainly true that for a very long while, stretching back somewhere near the beginnings of "Cain-ish" behavior, humans have been able to destroy whole peoples and scourge the earth in a given locale. That was, and is, horrendous enough. But it is yet another order of magnitude when the same fingers "which hefted the axe and won for us against tiger, bear, and ice" (the phrase is Loren Eiseley's) fondle nuclear triggers and gamble what has never been wagered before. That is not only life—and death—on unimaginable scale. It is, as well, the very *possibility* of future human generations.

We are hardly able to conceive what it means that sufficient human power exists effectively to end the life "experi-

21

ment." And we haven't begun to face what nuclear reality means for our most basic theological notions: of God, humanity, salvation, responsibility. (At least I know of no system of ethics, theological or otherwise, that does not simply *assume* that life goes on. Certainly no system of ethics has much contemplated the nature of a responsibility commensurate with the power to destroy that very assumption. This is one of the arenas that requires bold, imaginative, constructive revisioning of Christian faith.)

Thermonuclear reality encompasses far more than humanity, of course. As Hegel observed about the modern world, nature is increasingly "sucked up" into human history. In ever greater measure human power shapes both human and nonhuman destiny on and within range of this planet. Even someone so cautious as James Gustafson says: "The ordering of all life is shifting in a sense from God to humanity and doing so more rapidly in this century than in all the previous centuries of human culture combined."[4] The "ordering of life" includes the ordering of death on an immense scale. Such are the novel range, objects, and potential consequences of human power at the terminal end of the life spectrum.

At the front end sits another case. It is the capacity to author life and to intervene in ways that skip all over the genetic alphabet. Decoding the genetic code, unraveling the DNA molecule, is a power akin to atom splitting. "Biotechnology" may be a new word in the vocabulary of social responsibility, but it is an awesome reality even in its infancy. As one Nobel laureate has put it, "now we can outdo evolution."[5]

There are novel objects and consequences here, since we are considering potentially deep modification of current species and even creating new life forms. (These, the U.S. Supreme Court has ruled, can be patented and marketed.) What go unanswered, however, are the moral questions. Ethics pushes to the fore again. Who rightly possesses and wields such fateful powers? Who will be the "image-makers" and the decision-makers? By what standards will they envision and decide? Who grants the right to experiment on and for *future* generations of human and other life forms? How are the claims of deeply affected future generations registered in the present? How are the claims of both future and current generations adjudicated when they are in conflict?

There is genuine value, as well as shock value, in pointing to the ends of the life spectrum. Extremes force us to sit up and take note of a changed human world and its distinctive marks. This in turn begins to draw the lines of what socially responsible ministry must face and try to include.

But most of life isn't lived at the extremes. It happens in between, in the humdrum of small acts and in the accumulated good and evil routine. Yet in the modern world even routine acts accumulate large outcomes, not least because nearly five billion of us are doing the acting, with no new hemispheres to discover, settle, and exploit—at least not above water and on the ground.

What ultimately must carry the entire world of small acts is the natural environment, that "anvil" (Bacon) on which we hammered out the modern world. Although organization increasingly replaces nature as our immediate environment, as Bonhoeffer observed, the dependence on material nature is nonetheless *total*. And here the accumulation of small acts effects novel consequences across a novel range of objects. Nature is increasingly sucked up into human history.

We are, for example, responsible for the earth's future climate in a way previous generations were not, and did not imagine they would be. The negative effects on the ozone layer; the rise in carbon dioxide levels, threatening "greenhouse effect" for large areas; the unprecedented burning of fossil fuels, raising atmospheric temperatures (whether or not pollution is contained); the deforestation of the tropical forests (the "lungs" of the planet)—these are the outcomes of daily "small" acts that accumulate major consequences. No one group is "responsible" for these, yet together they create a condition for which responsible human action must be taken, together. Given the scale of human action now, the climate will no longer care for itself, at least not in ways we would find livable.

Long-held human assumptions are abruptly brought up

short here. The categories we think *with,* as contrasted with the things we merely think *about,* are often obsolete.[6] Consider these words by the nineteenth-century poet Gerard Manley Hopkins:

The world is charged with the grandeur of God.
   It will flame out, shining like shook foil;
    It gathers to a greatness, like the ooze of oil crushed. Why
does man then now not reck his rod?
Generations have trod, have trod, have trod;
  And all is seared with trade; bleared, smeared with toil;
  And wears man's smudge and shares man's smell: the soil
is bare now, nor can foot feel, being shod.
And for all this, nature is never spent;
  There lives the dearest freshness deep down things;
And though the last lights off the black West went
Oh, morning, at the brown brink eastward, springs—
Because the Holy Ghost over the bent
  world broods with warm breast and ah! bright wings.

Without for a moment understating the astounding resiliency and fecundity of nature here celebrated, or denying "the dearest freshness deep down things," we delude ourselves to assume, any longer, that "for all this, nature is never spent." But that assumption is as old as human habitation. For the sake of viable responsibility, it must be altered.

The novel range, objects, and consequences of human power in the modern world, illustrated from the ends of the life spectrum and the carrying capacity of the everyday world, pose unprecedented circumstances for applied human knowing. With the possibility of novel consequences across a novel range, how do we learn what works? How do we test new ventures?

In simple or sophisticated form the modern method is essentially one of trial and error. This is a sound procedure, provided the failures are not catastrophic. Risks are inevitable, and there are always costs, sometimes high costs. But the errors, it is assumed, will be corrected to provide an eventual balance of benefits over costs. The errors, it is also assumed, do not incur mass devastation in the process of experimentation.

But what if human power is such that the planet or some major portion of it is the laboratory itself? What if the outcomes are hypothetical *on a grand scale* and the laboratory isn't a contained, artificial construct?

We have, for example, "decided" to use fossil fuels on a grand scale. We don't know at what point the heating of the near atmosphere from their use will mean major climatic changes. And we cannot use trial and error to find out.

We have inspection methods for nuclear arms and we build massive systems to deter their use. But we don't know for certain that they will not be used. And we cannot test whether the scenarios of "nuclear winter," for example, are correct projections or not. We cannot, that is, use trial and error.

We know that releasing chlorofluorocarbons into the atmosphere damages the ozone layer. We don't know how many can be released before decisive atmospheric damage is done. And we can't use trial and error to find out where the limits are.

In short, human power now exercises risks that are global in scale and far-ranging in consequences, for both the short term and the long. It is probably true that there isn't any way to make most decisions apart from *some* degree of trial and error. It is also true that, in many cases, there is less and less room for error, and for saving correction. When the planet, or some major portion of it, is the laboratory, trial and error is severely altered. Socially responsible ministry must recognize that we now work with awesome possibilities and heightened risks.[7]

The description thus far has omitted discussion of the *institutional* character of society today. I have described the prominent and distinctive mark of the age as the novel impact of human power, but I have not said what the major *mode* of human action is. I have not described the dominant social form that channels human power. Any discussion of socially responsible ministry is obviously remiss if it omits the social media of power.

Here I can only be sketchy, and use shorthand to introduce an extended subject. The shorthand is to add Max

Weber to Bacon, Marx, and Freud and thus finish the composition of the modern quartet. And even here, only Weber's discussion of bureaucratization and rationalization will be lifted into view. In one complicated sentence it is this: in an environment that is more and more "organization" and less and less "nature" in a direct sense, organizational means will be adjusted to organizational ends in the most economical and efficient way; and the justification of authority in this process will be *via* knowledge used as manipulative power for achieving those organizational goals. This rationalized, bureaucratic pattern holds whether the scene is the marketplace and corporations, government, or seminaries, including the curricula of the latter. Members of an organization have standing if they can efficiently deploy a body of knowledge for the purposes of controlling behavior toward institutional goals, or at least if they can convince others that they control access to such knowledge! This is the bureaucratic and managerial mode of controlling the environment in rational ways. ("Rationalization" here means a division of knowledge and labor into specializations linked together as efficient means toward desired ends.)

The point is not simply to cite mass organization as the primary medium of human action today. It is also to recognize that little effective movement toward power, nor any major maintenance of power already attained, can be sustained if it does not take on this character. This pattern of rationalization may well have begun only in the case of the production and distribution of *goods* in the industrialized world. It has now clearly been extended to *services* and to *ideas* as well.

This is the summary, baldly stated: Bacon, Marx, Freud, Weber—whether as mastery of nature, society, or psyche, scientific knowledge and technique are the keys to power; power is used for control; and the dominant way of exercising power and control is by way of the rationalized systems of large organizations.[8]

Still such a bland description fails to note what I've tried to underline overall: our age is marked by quantum leaps in human knowledge and power sufficient to effect a novel range, novel objects, and novel consequences.

I add this sketch of the distinctive traits of a technological age to the earlier sketch of a world that shows the political fervor and religious vitality of struggling peoples and emerging movements. Together they strike the accents of the late twentieth century. They constitute the world that any normative view of socially responsible ministry must take account of.

The Church's Public Roles

The seminary's task of shaping socially responsible ministry in such a world depends on the church's task and, to a somewhat lesser extent, the university's. What is the role of the church, or the roles, from the perspective of Christian ethics? However such roles are conceived, they are certainly *public* ones now.

But what does "public" mean? "Public" here refers to a vision and understanding of our factual interdependence, despite the reality that most of us are strangers to one another and will remain so. (There are limits to becoming close friends with five billion persons!) "Public" means the realization that we strangers occupy a common earth space, share common resources, increasingly share a common destiny, and must somehow find common ways to learn to live together. Learning to live together is our public vocation now more than ever, whether gauged from the perspective of emerging movements and struggling peoples, or from the perspective of the far-flung consequences of cumulative human action in a technological era.

With considerable force the ancient image of the world as an *oikos*—a single public household—now has empirical reality. *Oikos* can guide our sense of public responsibility. It vividly expresses the ancient Jewish notion of *creation as all things together,* in their relation to God.

Both the empirical and the visionary realities are nicely

27

captured in this "public household" image: *oikos* is the root for economy (*oikonomia*), ecumenics (*oikumene*), ecology, and steward (*oikonomos*). The material and managerial well-being of the public household (*oikonomia*); the promotion of the unity of its family as a single family (*oikumene*); the knowledge of the envelope of life the household is part of, and dependent on (*ecology*); and the trusteeship of the household (*oikonomos*)—these are dimensions of a public vision of and for the church in our time. Indeed, they pertain with equal force to any university that takes "universe" seriously in its vocation.

This image ratifies some key theological-moral notions in Christian ethics. "Neighbor," for example, is a universalized notion that includes "all that participates in being," to recall H. Richard Niebuhr's phrase. The comprehensive biblical view of "justice" and "peace" fits here as well: whatever is due, or required (justice) for the fullest possible flourishing of creation (peace). *Oikos* and "public" are, then, not only ways *to name the arena* of the church's vocation, and the university's. They are also a way *to envision creation* in this age (as a single public household).

But what are the specific public roles of the church? What does socially responsible ministry "look like" from this view, in this world? The public roles discussed here are three. I preface them with a note on the definition of "church" used in this discussion. The church is that community which exists to announce and give social form to what God hopes and strives for, for all creation, as this has been glimpsed in Jesus of Nazareth and experienced in the Spirit.

1. *A community of radical critique.* David Riesman once described the kind of communities our time needs, naming them "anticipatory communities." Such communities are "utopian" in the sense that they take risks for a future they will never see; and they engage in that thinking and action "which confronts us with great hopes and great plans," abjuring "the lesser-evil thinking which poses immediate alternatives" only. They dream grander dreams even as social constraints multiply. And from this removed place they un-

28

dertake, as a consequence of their utopian and "anticipatory" character, a critique of the current social arrangements.[9]

The church, by virtue of its identity as an eschatological community, living from what it anticipates as God's future for all creation, would come to the same roles Riesman describes. From an eschatological perspective it would, for example, subject all the going social arrangements to radical critique. They would be relativized, rendered as possibilities rather than as necessities. They would be seen as human constructs subject to change. And this would pertain not only to material production, governance, education, and family patterns, but also to the ordering of ideas themselves, including theological ideas. Any of these might be regarded as provisionally valid in its current form, but the validity is, at best, only that—provisional.

One public role of the church is, then, to voice this radical critique. Differently said, this is one of the tasks of socially responsible ministry. And whether one wishes to borrow the slogan of the young Marx, "the relentless criticism of everything that exists," or use the more explicitly theological one of the young Luther, *crux probat omnia* ("the cross probes all things"), the outcome is the same. The piercing light cast by the reign of God demands that what is illumined be named for what it is, and truth be spoken to power. Needless to say, such critique is directed inward as well. It is carried out in both the public arena and the church's own sanctuary. It is self-critique and it is world-critique.

We should add that the other "partner" of the seminary, the university, also has this role as radical public critic. Here the roles of church and university nicely converge in the formation of socially responsible ministry.

2. *A community of pioneering creativity.* Riesman's comments on "anticipatory communities" included not only critique, but also "nuts-and-bolts" efforts to give social form to new possibilities. This, too, is a public role for the church. That is, demystification is not all that is glimpsed in Jesus and played out in his parables and other teachings, or reflected in the way threatened groups responded to him and his move-

29

ment. His penetrating exposures of "this present age" (to anticipate Paul's language) were coupled with efforts to strike down the barriers between groups that were at enmity with one another across hostilities of religion, nation, race, sex, cultures, and class. This effort to forge a community inclusive of creation never ceases, and the borders between it and the wider world must necessarily remain rather fluid. The task itself is never finished because new barriers continually arise within both "church" and "world." But there is, in our time, a special relevance for *social experimentation* aimed at "planetary inclusiveness" and the dismantling of barriers of hostility. This is all the more compelling in a world where change is especially volatile as the world shrinks, and human power to effect all life grows daily. Thus a second public role is *to help pioneer community-creating social forms in this dangerous, "ecumenical" moment.* In the first instance this means that the church is to *be* such a community of experiments in inclusive community. Ecclesiology *is* social ethics here. And the seminary's own campus reality should, by virtue of being part *of* the church, reflect this role in its own social formation.

From a different set of arguments, the same case for the "universal" as for the inclusive can be made for the university. I will not pursue that here, but only mention that the notion of university does not, of itself, militate against a view of socially responsible ministry as one that fosters pioneering community creativity.

3. *A community with a preferential option for the suffering.* Here the distance of the seminary from the university may become obvious. But the church's calling dare not, on theological grounds, become distanced from attention to suffering.

Intriguing in the accounts of Jesus is his movement to the places where the flaws of human community are most obvious. There he calls forth power that the people did not know they had. *Amid* suffering of all kinds is located the *beginning* place for that empowerment which heals rather than violates. (I add that shared joy is also a place for an empowerment which heals rather than violates.)

Going to the places of suffering is, granted, not all there is to socially responsible ministry, or to the empowerment so much a part of it. But it is a necessary part. And it is a "preferred" part, both for a theological reason and for a strictly prudential one. The theological reason is that this is the pattern of God's own way as seen in Jesus. The socially prudential one is that unless those who suffer are included— and those who suffer most of all—human community continues divided, the social poisons spread, and the wounds of the body politic fester even more. And in our kind of shrinking world the attendant dangers are magnified.

In summary, socially responsible ministry means at least these roles: public presence that shows itself in radical societal and self critique; pioneering community creativity; and ministry centered in the flawed places of human life as that is manifest in suffering of all kinds.

Seminary Tasks

Seminary educational contours should take their form from the church's roles and the university's contributions to that enterprise. That means such elements as the following (an admittedly incomplete list).

Tools for radical critique. These are "theological" perspectives that press "eschatological" criticism. These are, as well, analytical tools and knowledge from the human sciences that expose and describe the going arrangements of the current age. Tools for critique also means cultivating abilities to listen to people whose experience is not our own. That experience is, by implication at least, usually a critique of our experience, since it carries different perspectives on reality as we have come to know it.

Conscious efforts to "experiment" as church and see the implications for the wider world. The seminary is *part of the church*, not an educational stop en route to "serving the church." It should therefore be one place where varied ways

31

of expressing "church" in a time of deep change are tried. In the first instance this is the bold revisioning of faith, to recall our earlier discussion from Troeltsch. That will take the form of bold *thought* first of all, since the seminary's educational task is its prime one, bolstered as it should be by the university. But Christian thought is heretical if it is "discarnate," if it is detached from community practice—in the seminary's worship life, its presence in the neighborhood, its governance structure, classroom exchange, and so on. Our earlier words about joining bold thought to community-creating religion at the base and edges of society also pertain to the seminary community, as does the preferential option for the suffering, and for the reason given—the seminary is part of the church. Indeed, all this enters the basic decisions about what is taught, by whom, for what, and accountable to whom.

Revisions of the curriculum to see things whole. I began by noting that everyone is involved in moral formation and thus has a part in forging socially responsible ministry. I also noted the kind of specialization and division of labor ("rationalization") that is characteristic of technological societies. This rationalization shows up in seminary curricula as well—in the form of "theological encyclopedia," and as disciplines, subdisciplines, and specializations in methods and subject matters even within subdisciplines. Yet the quest must be for a more inclusive grasp of the Christian life (and socially responsible ministry). And that means the quest must be for a curriculum that is better able to see the Christian life whole. Expanding Christian Ethics as a field is not the avenue of approach recommended here, despite the keen insight of Troeltsch that in a time such as ours, matters of ethics always press to the fore. Rather, a curriculum better able, overall, to envision things whole would, by its own force, move toward socially responsible ministry. The key to it all is the quality of the seminary community *as church*, in and for our time. Social ethics is ecclesiology, now.

3

Black Theological Education: Dilemma and Deliverance

Jacquelyn Grant

There is an African folktale that goes like this: One day a little African boy came home from the mission school and approached his father with puzzlement. "Why are you looking puzzled?" asked the father. The boy said: "Father, I don't understand it. At school the teacher tells us that the lion is the king of the jungle. It is strong and ferocious. But what I don't understand is that if the lion is so strong, why does the hunter always kill the lion in the end?" To which the father responded, "Son, until lions learn to write, that is the way the story will always end."

Certainly, until people exercise some degree of control over their own lives, their destinies will always be in the hands of others. And in a society that is based on a model of domination/submission, some people are always in control of others. Until victims in such a society are able to break away from the dominating and oppressive control of people in power, their destinies will remain in the hands of oppressors. The oppressors' control permeates all institutions of the society—government, church, school, and family. Consequently empowerment is not as simple as the oppressed learning how to tell and write their own stories. For those in power also have taken the authority to call the stories of the oppressed, non-stories. More specifically, their cultures and histories have been deemed nonexistent.

Unfortunately theological education has not been resistant to this oppressive view of reality. In fact, theological education has been in the vanguard of oppression. Following the lead of white theology, theological educators have done their work without challenging the structures of oppression. In so doing we have produced generations of graduates who, for the most part, have had little or no commitment to changing the social, political, and economic conditions of the poor and oppressed. The theological education system, then, has been a partner in oppressive structures. In this sense, theological education has always prepared ministers for social ministry. To the extent that ministers have remained neutral or silent on questions of racism, sexism, classism, ageism, and militarism, they have supported the existing social, political, and economic structures. The question for me is how do we structure our educational programs in order to produce graduates who are committed to liberating ministries, be they practical or scholarly. This is recognized as a serious problem, for the agenda and goal of status quo-controlled education is not liberation of the oppressed, but the socialization of them by the norms of the dominant culture. In providing the argument for his *Introduction to Black Studies*, Maulana Karenga points to the need to provide "severe and ongoing criticism to the established order of things in order to negate myths, mystifications and insubstantialities of traditional white studies on Blacks, society and the world."[1] To do this, he calls for an afro-centric approach to education, which "is essentially intellectual inquiry and production, centered on and in the image and interest of African peoples."[2]

Victims must begin by telling their stories and writing their books. But if these books and stories continue to be ignored or degraded in the educational and theological communities, what impact is there to be made? In the following pages I shall explore the dilemma experienced by some in black theological education as well as offer an assessment of what is necessary for deliverance from the dilemma. I shall show the struggles of one community to make a difference in the way the story is told and indeed in the way the story ends. In order to put the issues in proper context, I shall explore the following dimensions of the dilemma: (1) the dilemma as seen in black scholarship, (2) the dilemma as seen in black religious scholarship, and (3) the dilemma as seen in black religious institutions, especially in the black seminary.

The Dilemma in Black Scholarship

One of the major problems still facing the black scholar today is the issue of identity versus scholarship—that is, what to do with black identity in a Western context in which nonwhite identities are not considered appropriate subject matter for scholarly pursuits. Black scholars have dealt with this problem in many ways. Martin Kilson suggests three strategies used by black intellectuals in the past. Some black intellectuals chose totally to ignore identity and withdraw from any political activity or commitment on behalf of black people. Some chose the other extreme, total politicization, wherein issues of black identity and politics were considered intrinsic to one's intellectual calling. Still others chose to become the marginal people who divided their intellectual concerns between creative scholarly engagement and political activism.[3]

The options taken by black scholars were not unrelated to the fact that they were trained in a context of racial oppression. Nonetheless the question of relevancy of black identity has been debated for some time. Carter G. Woodson addresses the issue in his classic book *Mis-education of the Negro*. He identifies the crux of the problem as the racist educational system itself:

When a Negro has finished his education in our schools, then he has been equipped to begin the life of an Americanized or

35

Europeanized white man, but before he steps from the threshold of his alma mater he is told by his teachers that he must go back to his own people from whom he has been estranged by a vision of ideals which in his disillusionment he will realize that he cannot attain. . . . While being a good American, he must above all things be a "good Negro"; and to perform this definite function he must learn to stay in a Negro's place.

For the arduous task of serving a race thus handicapped, however, the Negro graduate has had little or no training at all. The people whom he has been ordered to serve have been belittled by his teachers to the extent that he can hardly find delight in undertaking what his education has led him to think is impossible. Considering his race as blank in achievement, then, he sets out to stimulate their imitation of others. The performance is kept up a while; but, like any other effort at meaningless imitation, it results in failure.[4]

What is quite clear in this commentary is that the education of blacks, even for the black community, is controlled by those outside the black community.

For Woodson the problem with the American system was that the normative white experience served as a built-in negation of the black experience. What is likely to be produced, then, is a black intelligentsia with little or no commitment to the black community.

Later, picking up one of the ways in which such racist practices in the American educational system affects some blacks, Langston Hughes begins in this way an article entitled "The Negro Artist and the Racial Mountain":

One of the most promising of the Negro poets said to me once, "I want to be a poet—not a Negro poet," meaning, I believe "I want to write like a white poet"; meaning subconsciously "I would like to be a white poet"; meaning behind that, "I would like to be white." And I was sorry the young man said that, for no great poet has even been afraid of being himself. And I doubted then that, with his desire to run away spiritually from his race, this boy would ever be a great poet. But this is the mountain standing in the way of any true Negro art in America—this urge within the race towards whiteness, the desire to pour racial individuality into the mold of American standardization, and to be as little Negro and as much American as possible.[5]

36

Hughes obviously perceives a direct connection between identity and artistic accomplishments. Identity impacts perceptions of reality. Further reflected in Hughes' comments is a questioning of the perception that one can really be great while denying who one is. One may receive fame and acceptability, but not real greatness. One could imagine Hughes reasoning that, in the first place, in a racist society, white people do not allow black people the luxury of forgetting who they are and, in the second place, one cannot do one's best while working under the limitations of pretentious living.

Racism affects both the racist/oppressor and the victim in a peculiar way. It makes oppressors believe that contained within their experience are the questions and answers of human existence, and it makes oppressed peoples believe the same. Consequently the oppressed become preoccupied with "being like those who are their oppressors." Unfortunately movement throughout the educational system of America does not necessarily reduce this preoccupation of black people.

For the inherent racism in this American educational system produces insecure black scholars. It produces scholars who have more faith in white intellectuals' capacity for analysis than in their own.[6] Harold Cruise analyzes the contribution of black leadership and challenges the creative intellectuals at the points where they have abnegated to white scholars their task of interpreting black life and culture. Challenging black Americans to stop uncritically borrowing and allowing to be imposed on them the cultural experiences of others, Cruise identifies the black experience as unique and therefore as a valid and necessary area for exploration by the black intellectual. They need not continue to play second-class citizens in the academy.

> The white intellectuals do not recognize the Negro intellectual as a [person] who can speak both for [black people] and for the best interests of the nation, but only as someone who must be spoken for and on behalf of. . . . There can be no real black revolution in the United States without cultural revolution as a corollary to the scheme of "agencies for social change."[7]

Simply put, what these scholars are arguing, although from different perspectives, is that black identity is an important factor in the development of the agenda of black people. Certainly it is a minimal requirement for authentic and adequate service to the black community. If this is true, then there is much to be said about the lacks in the educational system when it comes to the preparation of blacks.

The Dilemma in Black Religious Scholarship

The same challenges that confront the secular black creative intellectual also face the black religious scholar. Carter G. Woodson's commentary on what happens to blacks in the American educational system accents the fact that the system leaves some black intellectuals unfit to serve the black community because they are uprooted from their heritage and made to feel that their heritage is irrelevant to anything intellectual. I find Woodson's comments relevant to the American theological educational system as well. Theology and theological education, it was believed (and perhaps still is today), had nothing to do with the experiences of particular groups of people. Operative here is the assumption about the objectivity and universality of knowledge and of theology.

The rise of black liberation theology in the 60s challenged much of this, yet the belief lingers on. Perhaps this is why black theology remains on the periphery of theological curricula of most seminaries (that is, if it is in the curriculum at all). This belief in the unrelatedness of black identity/heritage and theology is further manifested in the large number of white religious scholars who can write about contemporary theology and not mention black theology. It becomes hilariously evident when books on liberation theology can be read as though black theology never existed.

As Hughes elevated the identity crisis of some black poets, the same crisis is evident among some seminarians and black religious leaders and scholars. This is reflected in two ways—at the level of self-identification and at the level of the identification of form and content of thought. Indeed that is why even today some will ask, "Why talk about black theology? Why not just theology—after all, theology is universal."

Cruise's sharp challenges to black intellectuals have significant implications for black religious scholars. The constant denegration of black religious studies in seminary curricula sends a message to seminarians that "real" theology is done and taught in the "real" curriculum, while those polemical, irrational thoughts are disseminated in the seminary ghettos of special and ethnic studies. One is left wondering what kind of psychological effects this message has on potential black religious scholars. Perhaps this, compounded with the continued racism in the publishing houses, partially accounts for the limited publications on black theology and the black religious experience, especially as compared with the proliferation of volumes in the areas of feminist theology and Latin American liberation theology.

The challenge of the black religious scholars is twofold: they must take seriously the community and the heritage that is theirs, and they must produce responsible scholarship that in addition to serving the needs of their community, can withstand the critique primarily of that community. They must strike that delicate balance between creative engagement and political commitment. With this balance we leave behind all notions of intellectual gymnastics for the sake of exercise, art for art's sake, or theology for theology's sake. What is most critical is the ways in which intellectual engagement serves the community that nurtured and sent forth people to be scholars.

The Dilemma in Black Theological Education

In describing the task of the African seminary, an African professor said to me, "We are no longer interested in theological education in Africa; we are interested in African theological education." Similarly, black theological educators need to move away from discussions that center around theological education and the black experience, and explore farther black theological education. Charles B. Copher in 1970 articulated what is required for seminaries to take the black experience seriously. He said that several things must occur.

1. The discovery and reclamation of a black heritage that has been lost, unrecognized, or ignored as an entity of little or no value.
2. The development of a sense of dignity and worth, and of pride in the black heritage on the part of black people.
3. The increase of knowledge and the development of skills that will free black people from oppression and dehumanization, and enable them to survive in an unjust society.
4. The informing of white people of the black heritage toward the end of changing attitudes for the better, and of liberating white people from false notions.
5. The investigation and analysis of the black religious experience toward the end of discerning its liberating and life-sustaining aspects for the benefit of both black people and white people.[8]

What Copher recommends here is *minimum* for taking the black experience seriously. The challenge for black theological education goes a bit deeper. The black experience must not only be taken seriously by black educators, but it must also be their raison d'être. It must be the context out of which the critical questions for black theological education emerge. They cannot remain content with the theological questions (and answers) being raised outside the black community and being imposed on them to be learned and repeated on examinations. Rather, they must be on the cutting edge of theological developments.

We at the Interdenominational Theological Center (ITC) have taken strides in this direction; we still have work to do in this regard. We have said that our "primary mission is to provide quality theological education for the predominately

Black Christian Churches."[9] In light of this, our recently revised curriculum has made Black Church History a requirement for all students.[10] Even though Black Theology remains an elective, it is taught in the two core courses in theology. I do anticipate the time when this, too, will become a core course.

Certainly we have begun to take the black religious experience (and the black experience in general) seriously. In many of the courses particular emphasis is given to relevance of the subject matter to the Black Church and to the black community. Some courses may even result from the needs of the Black Church.

I contend that there should be a more deliberate effort to respond to the needs of the Black Church and community. When the challenges for seminary curricula come from the church and community, many opportunities will be created for the broadening of the narrow perspectives of seminary-related people. By so doing, in preparing its curricula and related programs, the seminary may find it more appropriate to develop relationships with schools of sociology, law, political science, and education, rather than just with schools of philosophy. But liberation theologians have already suggested that. The experiences of the people determine questions not only for theological reflections, but also for programmatic developments at the seminary.

The question for theological educators is how do we best prepare seminarians to change the dilemmas coming from the daily lives and experiences of people into creative and relevant opportunities for effective ministry? In the black community we still find many of the long-standing contradictions that stem from racism, the resultant classism, and the ever-present sexism. There we see

1. disproportionately high unemployment and underemployment;
2. consequently, disproportionately high numbers living in poverty;
3. inadequate education;
4. disproportionately high black male imprisonment;

41

5. disproportionately high black female-headed house-holds;
6. disproportionately high black teen parenting;
7. disproportionately high land loss, especially among rural black property owners;
8. poor health care;
9. inadequate housing; and
10. the draining of the black community by racketeer business people, and the poor business practices of black people themselves.

The list could go on and on. The point to be made is that an adequate analysis of any aspect of the condition of many in the black community should suggest minimally that most seminaries do not prepare students to deal with these issues in any significant way. Ministry is not guiding churches in "charity work." Soup kitchens and clothes closets are commendable for addressing immediate crisis needs. But they do not address the larger and deeper issues of unemployment and underemployment. Ministry cannot be limited to preoccupation with only symptoms, but must move beyond that level to causes.

Deliverance from the Dilemma of Black Theological Education

I began with the story of the fate of the lion when only the hunter has the skills, the power, and therefore the "right" to tell and write the story. This so sharply depicts the situation of any oppressed group of people. From there I moved to a discussion of the parallel dilemmas of black scholars, both secular and religious, when they indeed have been trained to write, but have not yet been given the freedom to write without fear of rejection because of who they are, or without fear of reprisal if they should write from their own perspectives and experiences. The key is not in just learning to write books, but in doing so free from the control of oppressors.

Black institutions of higher learning naturally would suffer from the same problem. The dilemma could be described as one of reputation and respectability versus relevance. Sometimes black scholars and institutions are caught in a bind. Is the lead given to white academic interests, or to the black community's lived realities? What is needed is a healthy balance. The balancing process can begin by bringing black studies up from the ghettos, in from the periphery, and into the main curriculum. Minimally this must happen in white seminaries.

I am suggesting that in black seminaries, because theology is reflection on the Black Church's and the black community's testimonies of God's activities in their lives, the theological curricula must be primarily defined by that reality. Thus we will no longer be concerned with theological education and the black experience, but with black theological education.

When lions write and tell their stories, not only is the end of the story impacted, but the content as well. Black people have always told their stories. Those stories have not been deemed proper sources for theological reflections. With the advent of black theology as a discipline came the affirmation of the black experience in general and the black religious experience in particular as sources for doing theology. Unfortunately, even when black theology is taught in the seminaries, it is usually lodged exclusively in the theology department. What is needed is an interdisciplinary treatment of black theology. Resources for this have been developed in such areas as Bible, church history, pastoral care, and sociology of religion.

Resources in these and other areas are minimal requirements for producing black religious scholars with a liberating perspective who could in turn provide the continued expansion of the reservoir of black religious resources. A people cannot be liberated as long as the resources for intellectual and moral development are produced only by the oppressors. (Between the lions and the hunters, lions always lose.)

Deliverance from the dilemmas of black education, secular and theological, lies with the degree to which two things happen. Because I've argued that theological education must

43

be the best yet be relevant, (1) we must redefine what it means to be "the best," that is, we must redefine excellence; and (2) we must recommit ourselves to relevance. Both requirements represent different sides of the same coin. The best in black theological education must be relevant. We can no longer afford to import the oppressor's understanding of excellence because excellence for oppressors can be detrimental to the health and existence of oppressed peoples.

As long as hunters write the story, lions will always experience premature death.

4

The Urban Ethos of Seminary Education

Ronald H. Stone

The particular social situation of a seminary provides a context for thinking about the possibilities and limits of theological eduation for social ministry. Many of our seminaries are regionally based schools. This chapter investigates the social location of a particular urban seminary, Pittsburgh Theological Seminary, in light of my thesis that social ministry education must take the social location seriously.

For this seminary the social location is a particular city. The students basically come from a three-state region dominated by the urban reality of Pittsburgh. Most of them will serve in the three-state region of West Virginia, western Pennsylvania, and eastern Ohio. The faculty live in and are influenced by Pittsburgh. The financial support of the seminary depends on relationships within the region. The minds of entering students reflect the social reality, including the Christian tradition as it has been imbedded or aculturated by this region. Their theological education occurs in the city, and for three or four years they learn theology and practice ministry there. The struggle to increase the social ethical sensitivity of students at the seminary is a struggle with this social reality. It is hoped that in my reflecting on the ethos of seminary education in one regionally oriented seminary, others reflecting on social ministry education can see the need for particularized, socially oriented reflections on theological education.

In Pittsburgh, slogans vie with one another to control the definition of the city. Alternative interest groups push their slogans: "Steel City," "Someplace Special," "City of Champions," "Renaissance City," "Third Largest Corporate Headquarters in the United States," "City of Neighborhoods," "Most Livable City in the U.S.A.," etc. Part of the meaning of the city is caught in each slogan. Obviously defining any city is a complex undertaking. Pittsburgh is both a unique city and a representative of a type of city. There is only one Pittsburgh, but there are many industrial cities in northern United States.

Roberta Ezra Park has defined the city as "a state of mind, a body of customs and traditions and of unorganized attitudes and sentiments that inhere in those customs and are transmitted with this tradition."[1] This chapter follows this direction in urban theory and inquires after the dominant state of mind in Pittsburgh to which its citizens consent. In the mode of Max Weber[2] it asks what is the controlling value orientation that gives the city its defining characteristics. It seeks to understand the origins of the value orientation; demonstrates how, in the crucial decision to revitalize the central business district, the value orientation was decisive; and critically reflects on that value orientation.

The controlling value orientation could be called an ideology by Marxist scholarship. Jacques Ellul's type of analysis would label such a value orientation "the meaning of the city." Robert Bellah's earlier method of inquiry would identify aspects of our sought-after value orientation as "civil religion." He currently describes the collected mores of a society in Alex de Tocqueville's phrase "habits of the heart."

46

Following more in the mode of Max Weber, this chapter discusses the fabric of the value orientation of this particular city, its "ethos." Ethos seems more appropriate, since classic Marxist analysis is not too relevant to an understanding of late twentieth-century American cities. Ellul's analysis is rooted in a type of biblical scholarship that leads him into what, from an American perspective, seem to be unnecessarily pessimistic conclusions. "Civil religion," although suggestive, may be too general a category for the purposes of this chapter, and it may overemphasize the important variable of religious factors in the culture. In the ancient city, as studied by Numa Denis Fustel de Coulange, religion probably could be seen as a crucial factor in the constitution of society. Modern society has many important variables in the value orientation and so the term ethos seems better.

Ethos, as a defining category for the city, indicates the interrelationships of a variety of norms, value assumptions, and meaning systems.

> It [ethos] is the subtle web of values, meanings, purposes, expectations, obligations, and legitimations that constitutes the operating norms of a culture in relationship to a social entity. And when the undergirding structure is as complex as the city the task of merely defining the ethos is monumental.[3]

The value orientation of the city will reflect ultimate values, but the ultimate values may themselves be hidden. Contemporary urban life has tended to obscure the values of the modern city. Some have found the ultimate values so hidden that in their search for the ethos of the city, they have focused on its secularity. Harvey Cox, for example, celebrated the secular politics of the city, its pragmatism, its anonymity, its disenchantment with nature, and its contemporary leaders. The secularity of the modern city even dominated the title of his study—*The Secular City*.[4] If, from the perspective of Pittsburgh, the celebration of secularity seems premature, his search for a definition of the city as a value structure was well intended and appropriate. The values of the city may not be obvious in contemporary America, and the methods of both history and sociology will be needed to uncover their meaning.

Max Stackhouse argued that "every urban center in history has had a theological principle at the core of its ethos."[5] Although perhaps the contemporary city is different, the theological principle of previous cities could be seen in the central expression of their architecture. In Mesopotamian civilization the ziggurat dominated as a temple. In Mayan architecture the pyramid temple was central. In medieval Europe the cathedral was the center of life, as the white church on the village green expressed the values of New England. It may be that the autonomy of the economic realm from religious influence in contemporary society will eliminate the religious values from dominant architecture. In the early nineteenth century the skyline of Pittsburgh was dominated by church spires. Gradually the buildings of the nineteenth-century individual entrepreneurs began to dominate the skyline. For a period the tower of the county courthouse, designed by H.H. Richardson, may have symbolized the new importance of the legal, bureaucratic society. Now, however, it is the corporate giants of the insurance companies, Pittsburgh Plate Glass, Mellon Bank, Alcoa, and most grandly United States Steel and Rockwell International that dominate the skyline. The church spires are lost in the crowded edifices of these new centers of influence, and a search for the ethos of Pittsburgh will have to comprehend the values of the transnational corporation.

A complete look at Pittsburgh would show how geography, forests, rivers, coal, and oil had a lot to do with how Pittsburgh developed. Geography for defense and control was central to our development. George Washington regarded the Point as the best place for a fort. His choice here was more propitious than his selection of the site for Fort Necessity, which he had to surrender. The geography still influences and defends the uniqueness of the neighborhoods and fragments attempts to plan or control the metropolitan area. National crises and forces of empire had their effect. We will find an exciting, dynamic-changing society. Renaissance I, after World War II, was a brave experiment in urban salvation, and now Renaissance II is reshaping the skyline. Yet, despite change, there is a great deal of continuity. These changes and the continuity both reflect value systems. Some of the changes were resisted. Sometimes battles were fought in the streets by competing groups. But consensus and change, with the population consenting to the change, have been ongoing features. The consent of the population reflects their sense of what is tolerable and what is valuable. People have given their energy to make this city, and they haven't done that for money alone; their sense of vocation and worth has also been involved. These commitments to certain values, certain styles of vocation, specific views of worth, and consensus as to how much pain is tolerable are included in the meaning of the *ethos* of this city or any other city.

Max Stackhouse, in his book *The Ethics of Necropolis*,[6] shows how the contemporary military-industrial complex has evolved with the expansion of urban civilization in America. He sees the military-industrial complex participating in the ethos of urban America. The urban ethos is characterized by

1. the dominance of human artifacts over nature,
2. a commitment to planning and management of human and natural resources,
3. the ability to transform the environment and human society,
4. technological capability,
5. population density, and
6. monied economy.[7]

In America these characteristics are expressed in terms of commitments to a view grounded in value assumptions drawn from the Protestant work ethic and social Darwinism.

In Stackhouse's view the emergence of the military-industrial complex, as it, through formal and informal relations, controls 10 percent of the population and the gross national product, has created a center of urbanized society that "appears both to be necessary for its preservation and to be the bearer of its death and destruction, the netherworld of Protestantized modern society."[8] So we are living in a necropolis; our social organization threatens our death. The ironies are deep: to defend laissez-faire capitalism, the military is the largest socialized force in our society. To defend freedom, freedom is sacrificed in the internal mechanisms of the complex. To defend urban culture, the military drains the urban centers of the money they need for renewal. It uses the highest products of our culture, not to advance the culture, but only to preserve it or maybe bury it.

Pittsburgh participates deeply in this ethos of the industrial-military-urban complex. In its universities it adds the educational element to the complex. It is a city of heavy industry, energy (coal and nuclear power), high technology, and firms heavily into the production of the technology of modern weaponry. At one end of the city is the Point, with the old fort of William Pitt. So the city is named Pitts-burgh, the fort of Pitt. At the other terminus of the central business district is the United States Steel building, housing Rockwell International, which is at the center of nuclear weapons development. Other major firms, Gulf Oil (now a subsidiary of Chevron) and Westinghouse, have competed for the control of the price of uranium. In the acropolis (high place of the city) may be the necropolis (tomb of the city).

The values in this most Presbyterian of American cities reflect the mixture of social Darwinism and the Calvinist work ethic. The search for the ethos of Pittsburgh will explain the reinforcement of the military-industrial-educational-urban complex by this mixture of social Darwinism and the Calvinist work ethic.

The Weber Thesis and Pittsburgh

In the 1970s I presented a series of lectures on social ethics in Pittsburgh to a lay education class in a prominent Presbyterian church in Pittsburgh's East End. The lectures were critical of representing the Protestant ethic solely as the ethic of law and hard work in one's vocation. The theme of the lecture series was that the classic Christian ethic, which stressed the three virtues of faith, hope, and love, was superior to the truncated presentation of Protestant ethics as the work ethic. A leading, highly educated layman referred to the ethic of faith, hope, and love as a "Hippie ethic." The response revealed how far the work ethic had gone in dominating the minds of Presbyterians in Pittsburgh.

It is often said in Pittsburgh that although John Knox prayed only for the establishment of Calvinism in Scotland, God threw in Pittsburgh also. Pittsburgh is not numerically Presbyterian; the Pittsburgh Presbytery includes only approximately 87,000 members. But in the history of Pittsburgh, Presbyterians have, to a remarkable degree, controlled the material system of production and, in alliance with work ethic Christians of other denominations, set the rules of the city's business community and many of its other institutions. The work ethic of Calvinism has been one of the major ingredients of the Pittsburgh ethos.

Samuel Schriner's novel *Thine Is The Glory* is the story of a Scottish family named Stewart, whose characteristics reveal a common set of mind shared by many of the Scotch-Irish families who came, in the nineteenth century, to shape Pittsburgh. The family, in the first generation, is represented as portraying the virtues of the work ethic. The patriarch of the family has a concern for honesty, and his self-discipline borders on asceticism. He is religiously and economically self-assured. He scrupulously keeps records while being imaginative in sensing business opportunities. His life is a rational search for profit making, and in his search for profit he is relatively undeterred by compassion for those his business activities affect. The second and third generations of the patriarch's family are less interested in business, however, since that was their parents' life. They rebel against the asceticlike discipline, become enamored with culture and the arts. They are even less interested in Presbyterianism, and some become Episcopalians and some become secularized. Schriner represents the older family as enjoying the saying "Even in business the Lord's blessing upon those who serve him."[9]

It is part of the folk wisdom that being religious produces prosperity. Most pastors know of prosperous families who attribute their wealth to their practice of giving a tithe to the church. A countertrend less frequently found is of the family whose generosity, based on religious motivation, has led them into bankruptcy. Reinhold Niebuhr liked to balance the tales of the successful tithing businessmen with reference to the shopkeeper who, in the Depression, overextended credit so that families could have groceries. He lost his shop.

John Wesley's experience was that religion of his type of disciplined evangelical piety helped the downtrodden to become prosperous, but that then their prosperity undercut their piety. Experiencing over his lifetime the increasing prosperity of his followers, he urged them "to earn all you can, save all you can," but then he added, "Give all you can away." The very polemical name given to Wesley's followers of Methodists reflected their methodical, disciplined approach to life. In their rigor they were typical of an emerging type of religious life that Max Weber called intraworldly asceticism.

Max Weber, a German social economist of the beginning of the twentieth century, had tried to explain why life in the Western world was different from life in the Eastern world. He reflected on previous work that associated capitalism with Protestantism and particularly with the Protestantism tracing its origins to John Calvin and Geneva. He was especially fascinated with the rigorous discipline of the Calvinists that, as they evolved, made them particularly inclined to associate with the spirit of capitalism or the disciplined, methodical drive to work, to accrue profits, and to reinvest the profits to expand business.

He was not satisfied with explanations that the material system of the production of goods determined life. He sought to understand why certain systems of material production were legitimated and accepted within certain value systems. He found the special variety of capitalism that characterized the early twentieth century of the Western world to be unique, and he thought that its emergence and acceptance were reinforced by aspects of Calvinism. The economic practices were not determined by religion; nor was religion determined by economic practices, but in a certain constellation of factors they could reinforce each other. He found several aspects of seventeenth-century Calvinism's asceticism that he regarded as supporting the spirit of capitalism. The ideas that faithful labor was pleasing to God and that, in the Old Testament, God was portrayed as rewarding people when they were loyal were helpful in inclining people to work beyond their immediate needs. The idea that the Christian was to reform the world and that secular vocations were as pleasing to God as were religious vocations strengthened the commitment to labor in a vocation. The idea that waste of time was sinful and even the wealthy were to work produced a mind-set of productive labor. The encouragement of the virtues of middle-class home life spurred the engines of capitalism. The teachings against worldly pleasure and consumption inclined those influenced by them to accumulate rather than spend. The polemic against dishonesty and avarice made it easier to engage in rational business organization.

Weber's attempt to correlate a tendency of certain Calvinists with a particular type of capitalism has been heavily criticized, and it is still the object of volumes of commentary and further research. If, however, the thesis is read in the subtle, careful way that Weber often protected it, it survives as a subtle correlation and mutual reinforcement of the two ideal types of the Protestant work ethic and the spirit of capitalism.

Weber was afraid that the values of liberal humanism influenced or engendered from Protestantism and the Enlightenment were threatened in the world emerging before and immediately after World War I. The combination of bureaucracy, capitalism, and the waning of religion was producing a technologically, bureaucratically organized society in which humanity was in danger of being lost. The decline of Protestantism was denying the culture its soul, and the disenchantment of the world engendered by the Protestant reforms was leaving humanity naked in the bureaucratic world that he labeled "the iron cage."

The third element in the Pittsburgh ethos is Social Darwinism. In the last three decades of the nineteenth century and in the beginning of the twentieth century, according to Richard Hofstadter, the United States was the Darwinian country. Social Darwinism, as taught by William Graham Sumner and Herbert Spencer, came to mix into the minds of the industrial magnates who controlled Pittsburgh. In their practice Social Darwinism justified the competition of laissez-faire capitalism, as well as utilization of the government, for the growth of their corporations and for protection from the workers. Its view of the world as a struggle for existence involving development over aeons reinforced their conservatism. As Spencer's philosophy was accepted, the will to reform was paralyzed.[10]

The previous synthesis of the work ethic and capitalism natural to the Scotch-Irish of the Ohio river valley adopted a social philosophy that taught that some were the fittest to manage the economy. The whole system in the hands of William Graham Sumner integrated the determinism of Calvinism with a scientific determinism that justified the way things were in a laissez-faire economy in which some Scotch-Irish were the rulers. Combining his theological training with the new social science, Sumner, "like some latter-day Calvin, came to preach the predestination of the social order and the salvation of the economically elect through the survival of the fittest."[11]

Of course, Social Darwinism undercut the very Christian faith on which the work ethic depended. But this undercutting was not generally perceived, and Christian faith lost its demand for social justice. Andrew Carnegie is an example of one Pittsburgh magnate who saw that his adopted Social Darwinism undercut his faith. On adopting it he gave up his form of Protestantism and evolved his own synthesis of religious universalism and Social Darwinism: "All the remnants of theology in which I had been born and bred, all the impressions that Swedenborg had made upon me, now ceased to influence me or to occupy my thoughts."[12]

Into this ethos the immigrants from central, southern, and eastern Europe were lured.[13] Into the factories they came. Catholic and Orthodox Christians were brought to work the fires of the industrial expansion governed by the Calvinists.

The fires caused Charles Dickens, on viewing Pittsburgh from Coal Hill (now Mount Washington), to describe the city as "Hell with the lid off." Out of this mix has come the ethos that still governs Pittsburgh today, as seen in Renaissance I and II, in which, during the New Deal, the Republican political machine was displaced by a Democratic political machine that finally, under David Lawrence and now Richard Caliguiri, could unite Republican business with Democratic politics to rebuild the downtown business center. The reality of this mix is caught in a comment of Catholic bishop Vincent M. Leonard to the new president of the Pittsburgh Theological Seminary. He said that he had 940,000 members in his diocese and that the mortgages on their houses and on many of the churches were owned by Presbyterians. But before we celebrate the city that the Renaissance turned around, we need to listen to a Pittsburgh historian describe the pre-New Deal, pre-Allegheny Conference on Human Development city, reinforcing the above analysis.

> The supreme crime in Pittsburgh . . . was "willful defiance of the little group of Scotch-Presbyterians who regard themselves as having been elected by Providence to be the city's masters, and who are in fact, its masters." Their economic and religious values had produced a civilization which was dull at best and otherwise barbaric. The city would benefit immeasurably from one large and comprehensive funeral—it needs to bury John Calvin so deep that he will never get up again. Dwight MacDonald conjured up the same image of a "big-business culture at its crudest and most powerful," tempered by a veneer of spirituality. Nowhere were the worldly needs of the average citizen more neglected and nowhere was there a more anxious concern for his spiritual welfare. Richard B. Mellon, brother of Treasury Secretary Andrew Mellon, had responded magnificently to the challenge of the depression in 1931 by announcing a gift of $4,000,000 to build the East Liberty Presbyterian Church.[14]

A sermon in East Liberty Presbyterian Church in the summer of 1986 asserted that one of the dangers to American society was the eroding of our individualism. Individualism—particularly the radical, almost ontological individualism that characterizes aspects of America's construct of social reality—is the danger, according to Robert Bellah. The research team who wrote *Habits of the Heart* found individualism to be a prevalent mind-set that thwarted the development of public commitments and public philosophy. De Tocqueville had, in the 1830s, found America characterized by biblical symbols and republican political discourse as well as by entrepreneurial individualism. In the 1980s it appears to these social researchers that individualism is America's success-oriented form, and that its therapeutic and expressive forms were supplanting biblical symbolism and republican political philosophy. Whether or not America could find a language to revive its voluntary association creativity and to surround its public life with articulate and compassionate discourse remained a pressing question.

Bellah's classic description of the American character has to be painted in more dangerous hues for Pittsburgh. Here the individual model is not the myth of a cowboy. It is a myth of the individual in work ethic and Darwinist terms. The entrepreneur gains all that is possible from each worker. The worker labors until the industrial pace sends him or her to an early grave. The system works best under wartime or now prewartime conditions of buildup. So there is a frenzy of effort to work and produce. The union qualifies the loneliness of the worker but becomes closed in on itself, protecting its members from the claims of other communities. Bellah's middle-class study does not directly illumine this reality of the unionized family in its ethnic neighborhood.

The Presbyterian churches of the city, dominated by middle-class values in membership and clergy, stress the individualist side of the Reformation, presenting in some cases almost pure models of work ethic mentality. Probably in most cases their reinforcement and legitimation of entrepreneurial individualism are not as dramatic as East Liberty Presbyterian Church, which contains the carved sarcophagi of two members of the Mellon family. But after seventeen years of teaching in Pittsburgh, it seems to me that the Presbyterian reinforcement of individualism is clearly dominant.

56

The Current Celebration

The new *Places Rated Almanac,* by Richard Boyer and David Savageau, has rated Pittsburgh as the best metropolitan area in the country in which to live. The survey included factors of climate and terrain, housing, health care, environment, crime, transportation, education, recreation, arts, and economics.[15] In surveying 277 metropolitan areas in 1980, Pittsburgh was ranked tenth in health care, twelfth in recreation, and sixteenth in the arts. The survey measured the population as 2,263,894, including Allegheny, Beaver, Washington, and Westmoreland counties as of the 1980 census. The lack of high crime and high housing costs also contributed to ranking Pittsburgh behind only Atlanta, Washington, D.C., and the North Carolina triangle as a desirable metropolitan area. In 1985 Pittsburgh had improved and was rated as the most desirable metropolitan area in which to live.

The only area rated as unsatisfactory in 1980, placing Pittsburgh 232d, was "personal economic prospects." The decline in the primary metals industry over the past fifteen years, accelerating since 1979, has been the major cause for this rating. Diversification into research, service, finance, and light industry has helped, but it has been inadequate to meet the need, and now only 24 percent of the work force is in manufacturing. All Pittsburgh is aware of the depression in the primary metal industries. In the 1985 report, housing and personal economic prospects were the areas in which Pittsburgh was rated as weak. Educational and health facilities were regarded as particularly strong, as was the availability of art. Other factors considered were rated as adequate, and so the city as a whole looked good compared with other American cities.

Although population loss for the metropolitan area is slight since the last census, the city of Pittsburgh has lost about a fifth of its population since the mid-1970s. This points to a mixed picture, increasing the tax burden on remaining population, increasing the proportion of low-income residents, and decreasing political clout. The remaining population is disproportionately poor and aged, as is the population of our inner-city churches. The city could, in 1986, still boast a governor and a U.S. Senator, but the area has suffered the loss of one congressional representative, owing to the population decline relative to the country.

Christian Social Problems

The number one threat to the possibility of a Christian life in Pittsburgh is nuclear war. The ethos of Pittsburgh supports preparation for the war in which Pittsburgh is a prime target. The ethos of militarization supports the feeling of anomie among the young and devalues the meaning of life. The community does not respond well to initiatives for peace-making. The cost of militarization is currently undercutting programs for the welfare of the population and impoverishing the population. Inflation and unemployment both have their roots in the cost of the military on the economy. Political and economic leadership seem unable to respond creatively to the increasing danger of the arms race and policies of confrontation with the Soviet Union.

Following close on the evil of militarism is racism.[16] Racism has led white Christians to abandon the city when confronted with fears about blacks in the schools. City churches decline with a migration caused by racial fears, and the churches have done little to help their members respond to their racism. Most Pittsburgh churches are either black or white, and resistance to neighborhood and ecclesiastical integration is still real. Efforts to break the cycle of poor education and unemployment for blacks have been sporadic and generally ineffective. The last major public push for black economic opportunity was in 1969–70. Some bright spots in Christian interracial work are known by all of us, but basically the task confronts us as it always has.

With reference to the schools, the election of three ministers (two Presbyterians and one Baptist) to the school board tipped the balance in an integrationist direction. For four years a black person has been elected chairperson on a board composed of three blacks and six whites. Ministers have also been on the forefront of helping to cool certain troubled situations, and a minister in the city's human relations commission has also worked on desegregating the schools and countering the Ku Klux Klan. The spirit of segregation receives new life from Washington, D.C., these days. Senator John Heinz's vote to deny bussing as a tactic for school integration is among the more recent blows to integration. There have been gains locally, however, and the ministers on the school board were clear about their commitments to counter segregation in the school system. Quality of education is also being struggled for under a new vigorous school superintendent. The word is out that the schools have to produce results. Still the city's ratio of 18.55 students per teacher and its expenditure of $1,523 per pupil are not impressive; such church programs as alternative integration and tutoring help, but the most significant church contributions have been the late—very late—contribution to the electoral process of integrationist school board members. The city suffers under the budget and philosophy of the current administration. This points to the third significant social failure of the church. Political apathy, ineptitude, and cynicism have been permitted to corrode the Calvinist commitment to political activity. The Calvinist tradition, from John Calvin, John Knox, and John Witherspoon, has been one of Christian political thought and action. The churches have retreated into pietism and sentimentalism and have refused to train members to see significant issues of social righteousness. This contributes to reinforcing attitudes of helplessness within the iron cage of modernization, which denies both individuality and social relatedness. Only a return to a Christian-informed political life-style can restore a sense of meaningfulness to the common and individual life.

The political dimensions of most of the Christian social agenda are clearly emerging, as is the resistance to prophetic or social ministry Christianity. The nomination of a Philadelphia minister for the U.S. Civil Rights Commission who opposes bussing for school integration, equal rights for women, and civil rights for homosexuals is an example of the political-religious alliance for repression. The nomination of a former minister who opposes human rights activity in U.S. foreign policy programs for the post of assistant secretary for human rights in the state department reflects the same insensitivity. Religious opposition to both helped to defeat their nominations. Economic opportunity and human rights both have a political dimension, and politics has a religious dimension that our churches have not been prepared to understand or respond to prophetically. In our system every two years the issues of Christian social ministry become focused in the electoral process. The relationship of faith to politics is a continual process, but it comes up for a renewed focus every two years in a crucial way.

The fourth social problem to be mentioned is the feeble effort of our churches to recognize women in ministry. We are known nationwide for our failure adequately to respond to the reality of women in ministry. Until recently chauvinism had a place even in our own seminary. The students have defied church discipline on this issue and helped to mislead congregations to bolt from the work of Christ as represented in the Presbyterian Church (USA). Mixed with sexism have been an incredible precritical use of the Bible and a virulent anticommunism. Both seminary instruction and Presbytery discipline have been inadequate to preserve the unity and peace of the church. The Seminary has responded by engaging women as faculty, encouraging women students, criticizing misogyny, including books by women scholars in courses, and sponsoring conferences by women in ministry. We need more response by the Presbytery in placement, encouragement, retraining of male ministers, and discipline of chauvinism, and in response to issues of women in society.

The fifth area of concern is the church's feeble response to the task of social ministry. The social dimensions of kerygma, diakonia, and koinonia are notably lacking. The ethos of Social Darwinism and laissez-faire capitalism, reinforced by a work ethic Protestantism, evokes sanctions against the preaching of the Word, the servicing of the needs of God's people, and the formulation of Christian community that empowers God's people to be free men and women. The resistance to the *laos theou*, people of God, becoming free is high here. Social ministry must be taught, reinforced, and rewarded. In this ethos this requires an incarnational, an institutional response. Neither Christian Associates of South Western Pennsylvania nor the Presbytery has found a way to approach social ministry. Because Pittsburgh lacks a unified strategy and theory of social ministry its practice suffers. Out of this captivity the denominational leaders must lead.

A sixth concern is the unemployment problem with the decline of heavy metal and coke production. The announced unemployment figures hover around 7.5 percent. Actual figures are estimated at something twice that number, and of course many have moved away from the declining industrial base. The microethical issues of domestic violence, suicide, crime, alcoholism all relate to the unemployment. At the same time, with the declining tax base, social services to the suffering are reduced. The church's role to help the transition to alternative vocations is at issue here. A small Lutheran-based group, the Denominational Mission Strategy, has attempted to resist, using dramatic protest tactics, the decisions to shut the mills. Such actions were rooted in social naiveté and the extreme pain of industrial workers. They failed. Other significant programs of relief have been mounted by various churches and coalitions of churches.

A seventh reality deserving of church focus is the aging of the city's population. Urban churches, or at least those in the inner city, are characterized by an aging population. Pennsylvania, and southwestern Pennsylvania in particular, has a higher percentage of aging population than the national averages. The adjustments to be made in preparing ministers to meet the realities of an aging population deserve exploration.

The Seminary Curriculum

Because the analysis of the seminary's curriculum is part of the larger project of "Theological Education for Socially Responsible Ministry," it is not undertaken here. One point of strategy for the education of ministry must be highlighted, however. Pittsburgh Seminary's struggle to counter the mind-set of work ethic, militarism, and Social Darwinist individualism is due to the possibility of having four required courses in a heavily structured curriculum. This depends on the decision of the seminary faculty to foster social ministry in two relatively distinct areas. There are two required courses in Church and Society. The junior course emphasizes urban sociology and Christian ethics. The senior course emphasizes Third World Christian social issues and peacemaking theology. The required ethics introduction, taken in either the junior or the middler year, emphasizes the history of the Christian ethical tradition and methodological issues, particularly the concepts of love, power, and justice. There is also a required course in ethics, which is taken from the elective offerings of the department.

The reality of this core curriculum of four courses inclines students toward electing other courses in the church and society and ethics areas. It also reinforces the concerns of social ministry by students and faculty in other fields. Other faculty offer electives in their own areas that complement those given in the areas highlighted in this chapter. For example, there is a regular offering of Peacemaking in the New Testament and a course titled Old Testament Ethics. In theology the courses on the Theological Ethics of Karl Barth and the course on Love and Justice deserve to be mentioned. Electives on Group Process and on Women in Church and Society are invaluable. The new course on Advanced Studies in Church and Society, by the Urban Institute of Pittsburgh, provides the best opportunity for dealing with urban racism. Other electives in business or economic ethics each year enrich the program.

The doctor of ministry program has required ethics courses in each of its distinct tracks. The Reformed Theology track of this program requires two specially designed ethics courses: one on the history of the transforming character of Reformed ethics and one on contemporary social policy issues before the Presbyterian Church.

Special Projects

Three institutionalized projects have impacted the Seminary's life and curriculum. The Peacemaking Program of the Presbyterian Church funded a year of emphasis on peacemaking at the Seminary. Special colloquia with outside speakers were held for the Seminary community, faculty meetings discussed the integration of peacemaking concerns into all courses, and attempts were made to change from world studies in biblical languages to an interdisciplinary course taught by professors of philosophy of religion and Old Testament. The emphasis built on an already strong peacemaking thrust at the Seminary, and a final colloquium was held for professors and administrators from other Presbyterian seminaries. Unfortunately the arms race, or stampede, continues. As I write, students down the hall are laying plans for their peace and justice week, focused on Central America.

A professor from the Iowa State University has been engaged as a consultant on the "Church and Aging." This is a three-year program in which the consultant engages with all faculty on issues of aging as represented in their own disciplines. With the cooperation of the Pittsburgh Presbytery and the national agencies of the denomination he also offers elective and D.Min. courses on the "Church and Aging."

A third important emphasis has been the development and funding of a Center for Religion, Business and the Professions. The Center with staff and budget unites the outreach programs of the Seminary in ethics with doctors, business people, and lawyers. Since the early 1980s the program of conferences on religion and business has been expanded to monthly meetings with business leaders, seminars through the Allegheny County Lawyer's Association, and conferences on medical ethics with the medical community of Pittsburgh. The new Center scheduled six conferences on issues of church and society for the 1987–88 academic year. The increased emphasis on continuing education spreads concerns of social ministry to clergy and laity who are seeking more education.

Conclusion

The social forces in the urban setting of Pittsburgh are heavy. Because they are present in the governance structures, in the students, and in the faculty of Pittsburgh Theological Seminary, no transformation to a complete form of education for social ministry is anticipated. A social ethic seeking justice for the society that is rooted in a theology of faith, hope, and love will remain in tension with the society. Students will learn that the purposes of the church are to make known the message of God's love and to serve the people so that love of God and love of neighbor will increase. But the translation of that love into vital ministries of koinonia, diakonia, and kerygma will be limited by the culture.

Individualistic interpretations of Christianity will continue in the curriculum despite the best efforts of those with a social vision to transform them. Social interpretations of church history, theology, and Bible do not prevail on the faculty, nor can they in the near future. The Seminary has not yet developed a program to integrate goals of a socially responsible ministry with field education.

The development of an urban institute at the Seminary in conjunction with the Presbytery, social service ministries, and urban planners from the University of Pittsburgh is in an early stage. It suggests the possibility of better education in urban reality, analysis of social systems, and more thorough connections with local congregations and agencies.

The real world of theological education is a competitive world of each discipline struggling for its place. Therapeutic individualistic models for dominance in the life of the seminary will not prevail. Models striving for biblical and classical language dominance have not been accepted. Models based on an overall social ministry paradigm cannot succeed either. Or at least they could not succeed until the society and the church were changed.

The cruel aspects of the individualistic culture can be combated and fresh compromises with it reached that will equip students to criticize the society and engage in social ministry as well as institutional maintenance of the church.

The Advisory Council on Church and Society's project on the church and social policy has identified four roles for any seminary of the Presbyterian Church. They are as follows:[17]

1. To be a center for theological reflection and engagement with the world on public issues
2. To provide assistance to the church's search for direction and policy on social issues
3. To prepare ministerial leadership that will sustain and guide the social witness of the church
4. To demonstrate faithful attention to the church's teaching on social issues in its own institutional life

Continuing attention to these four roles while building studies through curriculum development, and serious attention to the need for faculty in ethics, church and society, sociology of religion seem to me as an observer/participant to be a good task to attend to for the strengthening of theological education for social ministry.

5

Getting Our Priorities Straight
Theological Education and Socially Responsible Ministry

Karen Lebacqz

"Theology as pursued in the West has become a joke."[1] This scathing indictment seems an appropriate place to begin my reflections on theological education and socially responsible ministry. How I wish I had heard these words many years ago! How I wish I had heeded them! What pain I might have spared myself and my students if I had!

But although similar words have been spoken around the world for many years, I have not heard, and I have not heeded. I have gone on doing what I always did, teaching social ethics, participating in curriculum reforms, thinking I was engaged in training people for socially responsible ministry.

In truth, what I have been engaged in is cultural oppression. Unwittingly, to be sure, but nonetheless very assuredly, I have contributed to the construction of a form of theological education that has become, at best, a worldwide "joke" and, at worst, demonic. The result of a sabbatical leave in which I steeped myself in liberation theology and in the voices of the oppressed is a new perspective on theological education. My current research on professional ethics for clergy in the United States confirms some suspicions engendered by that leave.

The results of my reflections have been some profound changes in the structure and purpose of my own teaching. I will illustrate with reference to my introductory (and required) course in Christian ethics. I will then offer some theoretical justifications for the structure and purpose chosen for this course. These reflections have implications generally for the shape of theological education for socially responsible ministry. I will conclude with a particular issue that affects the structures of every theological seminary.

Christian Ethics: A New Face

The fall of 1986 has seen a complete restructuring of my introductory class in Christian ethics. In previous years I have begun this class with tools for ethical analysis: logic, syllogisms, ways of analyzing arguments, and so on. The students have then examined two "issues" in ethics: war and abortion. The juxtaposition of these two issues forces students to confront their own contradictions: pacifists who eschew killing in war but have no difficulty with it in abortion, and "just-war" advocates who permit killing in war but make no room for justifiable killing in abortion are both presented with their own inconsistencies. Logic and coherence of argument have been the primary goals as I struggled to help each student develop an ethical framework geared largely toward analysis of argument.

Consider by way of contrast the new approach.

Recognizing that despite recent faculty appointments and all the good efforts of the Pacific School of Religion to recruit minority and overseas students, we remain largely white, North American, and relatively privileged, I began this class with the requirement that each participant be exposed to voices of oppressed people. I do *not* mean that we began by reading liberation theology. Theology is the "second act." The first act is struggle. So we began with the struggles of people around the world.

Students could choose to read *Child of the Dark: The Diary of Carolina Maria de Jesus; Twopence to Cross the Mersey* by Helen Forrester; *Blood of the Innocent: Victims of the Contras War in Nicaragua* by Teofilo Cabestrero; *South African Women on the Move* by Jane Barrett and others; *Peasant Theology* by Charles Avila; or *The Gospel in Solentiname* by Ernesto Cardenal. All present real life, firsthand accounts of poverty, oppression, and struggle.

Only two questions were asked of these texts: (1) what are the causes of poverty and its related miseries? and (2) what is the role of the church in the light of the answer to the first question? These two questions frame our work for the semester. *All our subsequent theological and ethical reflections are being done in the light of these firsthand accounts of the causes and effects of poverty and its related miseries.*

Having heard the voices of pain and struggle, we moved to trying to understand the social circumstances out of which those struggles emerge, and the theological implications of them. In short, we turned to liberation theology. Specifically, we read Jose Miguez-Bonino's *Toward a Christian Political Ethics.* Here we confronted the importance of contextualism in ethics, and therefore of social analysis, as a tool for social ethics.

We then turned to one example of North American theology: John Howard Yoder's *The Politics of Jesus.* Yoder and Bonino were explicitly chosen as counterfoils, since each offers a "political" ethic and yet their approaches and conclusions are so radically different. It was my hope that students would think about the *political implications* of Christian faith and would come to see that every Christian ethic is a political ethic. It was also my hope that they would see how radically different an ethic is when done "from the Bible" in a relatively privileged situation, as opposed to being done "from the oppressed."

Each student was then required to choose two perspectives on theological ethics, representing different agendas. One perspective may be consonant with her or his own history and inclination; the other must present challenges to that history and inclination. Both perspectives must be relevant for the student's present and future ministry. They could choose from black, Asian, African, Latin American, Euro-American, or feminist theology. Special arrangements were made for those with special ministries: some are reading Native American theology and social commentary; others are working with gay and lesbian ethical reflections; one is working on Jewish perspectives. They are not permitted to do "case study" ethics, but are required to deal with the fundamental questions of method and perspective in ethics.

Students work on their two perspectives in small groups. Each student or group will write an essay; it will be critiqued, and they will then rewrite it or do an alternative project, such as a painting or a poem. All students will participate in a joint class venture in which we attempt to combine the different perspectives to see what collaboration among them might bring to ethical method and analysis.

This change is an experiment, and it seems to be working. Certainly I have never seen better small-group discussions in a class. Certainly the exposure to voices of the oppressed has already changed the way some students think. Others show a deeper appreciation for the "political" aspects of church and theology. To this extent, I think the class is successful.

Getting Priorities Straight

"Successful" at what? Why these changes? What is the purpose of the new structure? How do I assess theological education such that this new approach seems more "successful" to me? Let us examine the theory undergirding the educational experiment.

My year of sabbatical reading began with traditional philosophy and theology and concluded with immersion in liberation theology. That process of reflection convinced me that there is something central to the task of ministry, to the task of theology, and therefore to the task of theological education. At the risk of abusing an overused and under-defined term, that something is *praxis.*

By praxis I mean something akin to James Cone's definition: "a reflective political action that includes cultural identity."[2] Praxis is not pure social action, since it is "reflective" action. But it is also not pure reflection, since it is "political action that includes cultural identity." Praxis is that peculiar combination of action and reflection that emerges among people struggling self-consciously for liberation from oppression. Praxis is therefore not just every practice of the church. Nor is it merely exposure to poverty and oppression. Rather, it requires commitment to the struggles of the oppressed and dispossessed, and involvement in their cause of liberation.[3]

Praxis "comes before theology in any formal sense." Theological reflection is a "second act." Theology never comes first. Living and struggling and practicing justice—these come first. Theology arises out of the struggle, out of the practice, out of life. This is the proper order.

And this proper order has profound implications for theological education for socially responsible ministry. The proper order in which praxis comes first suggests a need for radical changes in method, structure, and vision in theological education.

Method. "The rational element, the logical element, the truth element, is always that the people may live."[4]

To accept praxis as the beginning point is to begin with a principle of "epistemological rupture."[5] It is to be open to brand new ways of doing, of thinking, of knowing. "We seek to foster a new theological rationality."[6] The very canons of rationality, logic, and proper approach to study must change.

For example, in classic academic theology "one is not supposed to introduce personal experience."[7] But in a theology founded on praxis the oppressed "begin with the study of our lives."[8] A praxis theology is understood as rooted in concrete human experience of God's actions in the world. The Word of God is heard in events, in particularity. Experience is the base.

Thus *methods* of study in seminary must change. Personal life and experience of injustice must be taken as a primary "datum" for theological reflection. Theology will come out of life, not simply out of books. Taking praxis seriously means understanding stories of pain and oppression as themselves theology: "If there's anything worth calling theology, it is listening to [oppressed] people's stories."[9] Classic theological method looked to scripture, tradition, and reason. It found the people largely irrelevant.[10] The new theological method will begin with the conviction that "the concrete truths of our lives, memories, and values are foundational to our conceptual work."[11] Thus theological method will change if praxis is taken seriously.

To suggest that theological reflection must begin with the stories of the oppressed is to raise difficulties for North American seminaries that are largely composed of those who are relatively privileged in the world. How do we begin with the stories of the oppressed if we ourselves are not oppressed? We cannot simply begin with our own experience if that experience is the experience of oppressors. Or can we?

Here several observations may be helpful. First, many people even in our privileged environment have had experiences of oppression. Although white women in North America may be oppressors in the world situation, they are oppressed in their own culture.[12] Others in the seminary will know sexual discrimination and oppression as gay men or lesbian women. There are stories among us that do indeed reflect the experiences of the oppressed. These stories can be used.[13]

Second, there are stories of oppression that have been recorded. A sampling of these is offered in the volumes cited above. Reading can be a form of "listening" to another, and therefore the use of books is not antithetical to encountering real examples of oppression.

Third, all people have had experiences of pain. Although not all would be "oppressed people," all may be able to link their own experiences of pain to the pains of the oppressed.[14] Thus, for example, in asking my class to read the stories of oppressed people, I trusted that the pains experi-

71

enced by the oppressed would in some way tap the pains among us. Thus, although praxis requires involvement in and commitment to the perspective and the struggles of the oppressed, it is possible to approximate some elements of praxis within a rather traditional classroom setting.

Praxis also means a new hermeneutics. A theology that begins with praxis takes its hermeneutical principles from the struggles of the people. The Bible is no longer merely an ancient text to be studied "objectively" or uncovered by historical criticism of biblical scholars. "Political commitment, informed by social analysis, provides an angle of vision that enables us to reinterpret the scriptures."[15] The implications of this new hermeneutics in the arena of biblical studies are worked out in some detail by Elisabeth Schüssler-Fiorenza.[16] Methods of biblical study will change if praxis is taken seriously.

A new hermeneutics—of suspicion and rupture—means the rewriting of much of our history. "We have to rewrite our history."[17] "Authentic black history is an investigation of the past through the eyes of black victims."[18] Feminists working out of a praxis approach talk about "herstory" rather than history.[19] In order to recapture histories that have been lost, new methods of historical study are needed: oral history, the use of poems and stories, an appreciation of art, and so on. Historical methods will change if praxis is taken seriously.

But most central for my purposes, since my field is social ethics, is the impact of praxis on methods in ethics. To take praxis seriously is to be open to the development of a new logic. "What is logical to the oppressor isn't logical to the oppressed."[20]

Oppressor's "logic" has dictated both the *content* and the *form* of the study of ethics. While the academic field of ethics has always tended toward social issues, in the popular mind, "morality" or "ethics" in the West has become largely identified with "personal ethics" (especially sexuality) as its content. Even when the academy tended toward larger social issues, it often adopted methods that undermined any direct approach to the experience of oppressed peoples. For instance, the syllogism and logical deduction of conclusions from widely accepted premises have been dominant forms. The result is an ethics that is irrelevant at best and oppressive at worst: "At present, while our ex-seminarian may be able . . . to forward moral arguments for or against extra-marital sex, he is totally unequipped to help his people even breathe under the yoke of poverty."[21]

Praxis as the beginning point for ethics means beginning with different *content:* with poverty, economic hardship, work conditions, political repression, cultural repression, racism, sexism, and oppression of all kinds. And it means accepting a new *form,* moving toward a new "logic" in ethics: toward stories; toward a logic in which the truth is not rational deduction, but "life"; toward a people-centeredness that makes relationship more important than rationality. "[In Africa] it was not rules and regulations that mattered, but *life.* Here in Western Europe, I am afraid, it is the other way around."[22]

Cone argues that authentic *theological* speech arises "only from an oppressed community which realizes that its humanity is inseparable from its liberation from earthly bondage."[23] The same might be said about authentic *ethical* speech. Ethics is not therefore primarily rules or norms or principles or logical deduction. It is lifting up the voices of pain and oppression and joining the struggle for liberation. Only out of that struggle can an authentic ethical speech arise. It is for this reason that liberation theologians eschew the "norms and principles" approach to ethics so common in the so-called first world.[24] If praxis is taken seriously, methods in ethics will change.

This change is reflected in my class by the choice of voices of the oppressed as the beginning point for the class and by some changes in what I expect of students' essays. Poverty is taken as the central issue, but it is not divorced from the multiple social realities that surround it or from the particular voices of pain that cry out against it. Both the content and the form of ethics change with this beginning point.

Structure. "It's really like you're just lying in this cage. For me, it's been the most blatant sense of racism I've ever suffered. Usually that sense comes and goes; but at the seminary it's been constant."[25]

This student's reflection on the racism she encountered in seminary suggests that if praxis is to be taken seriously, not only must methods in theological education change, but underlying structures must change as well.

If genuine theology arises from an oppressed community, then our seminaries will not be doing genuine theology unless they reflect that community. Although we can approximate some elements of praxis in traditional privileged settings, we cannot do a genuine theology out of the pains and struggles of the oppressed when we all represent the nonoppressed. Studying our lives can be genuinely revelational "only as our theological schools become genuinely inclusive."[26] It is devoutly to be hoped that some day we will not have to use words like inclusive or multiracial to talk about structures needed for theological education. But currently those words are necessary.

This means that racism, sexism, and classism must be primary issues for every theological school. The *structures* of theological education themselves must be reevaluated. Racism, sexism, and classism remain realities in theological education. Sadly, the statement that the sense of racism is "constant" at the seminary might have been made about my classes. Like most seminary professors, I have known that I am "racist" by virtue of my upbringing in North America, but I have thought of myself as one who is open to learning and who has tried not to be racist.

Yet people of color remain largely invisible in my classes. Their life histories, their struggles, their perceptions have not been the base out of which I have taught ethics. Like other professors, I have expected them to assimilate and accommodate to a largely white middle-class perspective.

My racism was brought home to me in sharp relief by a black-identified woman[27] who accused me of never calling on her in class. Startled, I began to retort that she never raised her hand, and that I would certainly call on her if she did. And then reality came crashing in, as I realized that my class was so oppressive to her that she literally *could not* raise her hand. She had become invisible in my classroom.

And just as racism continues to permeate our structures in theological education, so sexism exists "as a universal system of marginalization of women"—within seminary as well as in various cultures and at all class levels.[28] It is partly because women—especially women of color—do not have power in the structures of theological education that scholarship has not changed and that methods of theological education remain woefully inadequate.

But perhaps accompanying racism and sexism is an equally central problem: the problem of hierarchalism.

> It is not surprising that a frightened little theological student becomes the authoritarian in the parish. When his [sic] pattern of behavior in the seminary is that of subservience to (white) [male] authority, it is natural that when he leaves the seminary he reproduces the same pattern in the parish.[29]

Our structures in theological education become models adopted by graduates and applied to their subsequent ministries. When we are hierarchical in our structures, we teach an important hidden agenda to our students—a hidden agenda that assumes the validity of hierarchy.

Hierarchical structures in seminary undermine the possibilities for any true "praxis" as the base of theological discourse because they set some up as the "experts." Paulo Freire calls it the "banking" model of education. Whatever it is called, it works on the assumption that there are some in the know, and that others "need" what those experts know. The life experiences of the people become irrelevant in the face of such expert knowledge.

Seminaries are structured on unequal power. Seldom do we understand that this structure itself might be the subject of study. "The system concedes nothing without demand."[30] Conflict is inevitable where power is unequal. Thus The Mud Flower Collective eschews the white peace-seeking philosophy of "education-through-friendship," calling such a philosophy a luxury.[31] Instead, oppressed peoples "work on the assumption that conflict and struggle are intrinsic to any collegiality."[32]

Education is not a neutral enterprise. Everything we do either supports oppression or works for liberation. The first task of education for socially responsible ministry is to examine the methods and structures of theological education itself.

This concern for structure has affected my class in two ways. First, I have insisted that students learn "black theology" from my black colleague on the faculty, "Asian theology" from my Taiwanese colleague, and so on. To the extent possible, I have brought into the classroom a more "inclusive" faculty than I am able to represent by myself. Second, I have made a conscious commitment to small-group work in which the life stories and social settings of the students can become part of the "datum" of ethical reflection. I have also worked *with* students in their small groups, seeing myself as an equal in the process. Moreover, every assignment I have requested of them I have also done myself, thus attempting to narrow the teacher-student power gap.

Vision. Ministry, in the end, depends on vocation—the church's and the person's—not training."[33]

The methods and the structures that we choose for theological education are in part an expression of our underlying vision. What do we see as the basic purpose of theological education? Whom does it serve? What model or paradigm best expresses its character, and hence its necessary components?

Too often I think contemporary theological education is modeled on an understanding of "professionalism" drawn too narrowly from contemporary interpretations of training for other professions. This is what Bruce Gilbard calls a "sterile" professionalism.[34]

At best, the professional model is appropriate. To be a member of a profession was originally to "profess" something central for human life. Professionals were to exhibit certain forms of commitment, dedication, and character.[35] At worst, however, the professional model has been narrowed and eviscerated of this concept of "profession." It has become a model of professional *training* based on assumptions about the importance of certain conceptual tools. Adoption of professionalism as the goal and model for ministry has resulted in the adoption of cultural values and images of education that undermine the praxis and the prophetic stance of the church.[36]

An alternative to the professional training model of education, and one that comes closer to praxis as the root, is *formation*.[37] Formation as a goal does not suggest the kind of professional specialization that plagues most seminaries today. Formation is not rooted in the acquisition of specialized knowledge, but in the development of perception and character. Formation also assumes an educational atmosphere designed to train *all* the people: "the conscious reclaiming of theological education by all the people of God."[38] Formation is an approach to theological training that is more consonant with "conscienticizing" or with a "minjung" theology—a theology of and by and for the people.

Formation is designed to create leaders of the people, not theologians of the establishment. It cares less about academic specializations and more about the student's ability to apply her or his knowledge concretely where the suffering is. In a study of twenty-two graduates of Drew University Divinity School, Janet Fishburn and Neil Hamilton found striking gaps between theological training and ministerial practice.[39] They argue that clergy are lacking in a base for practicing ministry with integrity. Biblical-theological resources are not tapped as the root for ministerial practice. "We judged that this was not happening because the habit of connecting theology and practice was never formed in seminary," they declared.[40] A professional training model of education does not connect theology and practice; a praxis, formation approach begins with practice and therefore never divorces theology from it.

"I have often wondered," says Basil Moore, "what a white clergyman with a middle-class white suburban congregation would have to say to a black ghetto congregation in Soweto."[41] What we need is a vision for theological education in which it is more important to know what to say to a black ghetto congregation in Soweto than it is to know what Barth and Bultmann and Tillich and Troeltsch said about theology, however important their legacy. We need a vision for theological education that takes praxis seriously.

Concern for the vision dimension has resulted in some changed goals in my introductory class. Although students still write essays and participate in some traditional, "scholarly" enterprises, my goal is not excellence in ethical analysis or scholarship as it has been traditionally understood. My goal is changed thinking. The student who tells me that he or she has learned how to critique what the newspapers say about Nicaragua is the student who tells me that I am doing something right. "Success" is not the perfect essay in ethics, but the changed perception about the world around us and with it, the changed mode of being in that world.

Scholarship: A "Litmus Test"

But as the previous paragraph indicates, getting the priorities straight raises some problems for traditional assumptions about scholarship. All these changes—in methods, in structure, and in vision—present problems for what we have traditionally understood as "scholarship" and as "excellence in scholarship." Our standards of scholarship are, in my experience, one of the most oppressive aspects of theological education.

In its searing analysis of theological education The Mud Flower Collective argues that "that which constitutes excellence or competence can no longer rest on knowledge about white male culture, or on an assumption of knowledge as detached from the life experience of the knower."[42] I agree with this claim. But I think it does not go far enough. Detachment and focus on white male culture are not the only important issues.

Elsewhere The Mud Flower Collective offers the following as criteria for the adequacy of theology: inductive, synthetic, and imaginative thought; perceptiveness, insight, depth and breadth of critical illumination; and respect for the diversity of experiences of people in different social locations.[43] Again, I agree. The scholarship that we seek to lift up as "excellent" scholarship must indeed present imaginative insight and critical illumination. But to say this alone does not touch the root problem as I see it.

What we need is a *requirement that scholarship arise out of praxis.* Thus scholarship must not only be inductive, perceptive, respectful of diversity, and so on, but it must also be rooted in particular experiences and commitment to the struggles of the oppressed.

To take seriously such a requirement would be to change radically the way in which we review faculty for promotion and tenure. "Excellence" in scholarship would no longer be judged by thoroughness of library research or demonstrated familiarity with all other positions taken on a topic. *Excellence would be judged by depth of experience in the struggle, by the ability to listen and hear the voices of the oppressed, and by the coherence of praxis and theoretical work.* If we took seriously praxis as the beginning point for theological education for socially responsible ministry, we would lift up different criteria for excellence in scholarship: involvement, passion, empathy, ability to relate abstract disciplines to concrete issues, and a "logic" rooted in "life."

Moreover, the judgment of scholarly "excellence" would have to be rooted elsewhere. Excellence would be judged not by scholastic peers, but by the communities of struggling people, the churches, the laity. Theological reflection would be "excellent" only if it spoke to the people: "The theology marketed in the seminary seemed ridiculous to me. . . . I said to myself, 'I don't know anybody who believes this.' "[44] Theological reflection would not be considered "excellent" unless it "makes a difference" for people's lives. The churches as well as the academy would therefore have responsibility for assessing scholarship. To suggest that the churches would be more directly involved in assessing scholarship is also to call the churches into accountability for the scholarship fostered in seminaries.

During the hours that I exist before my computer writing this essay, one of my colleagues is being reviewed and considered for promotion. Will his commitment to and involvement in the black community be considered an important part of his scholarship, or will it be seen as something that detracts from time spent in the library doing the necessary work for "excellent" scholarship? Will he be rewarded for combining biblical study with concrete pastoral concerns, or will his scholarship be considered too "interdisciplinary" and therefore "weak"? It is likely that he would be rewarded for sitting in front of a computer writing an essay demonstrating classic exegetical skill; it is less likely that he will be rewarded for his praxis engagement and commitment.

Just as women have so often been put in the position of being superwoman—having to work outside the home *and* still carry the traditional role at home—so I think today we expect of scholars from all oppressed groups that they will be superpeople—related to their groups and participating in the struggles for liberation of those groups *and* still carrying the burden of "proving themselves" in traditional scholarly modes. The criteria for "excellence" in scholarship remain traditional: thorough library research, demonstrated familiarity with classic modes of thought and analysis, clear and dispassionate presentation. Part of the reason that students in seminary do not develop the habit of connecting theology and practice is that such connections are neither required nor encouraged for faculty.

I have dwelt on the issue of scholarship and criteria for faculty promotion and tenure because I believe that it is central. Until we change the criteria for review and promotion of faculty, we will not change scholarship. And until we change scholarship, we will continue to have a theology that is perceived as a "joke" by oppressed peoples around the world.

Unfinished Agenda

My reflections on praxis as the beginning point for theology have resulted in some major changes in my educational approach and style. Yet, despite the striking differences in the introductory class from my previous efforts, I suspect that my new approach still represents only a halfhearted response to the "joke" of Western theology and ethics. I wish I could say that I have made "radical" changes, but my long years of traditional training and traditional work styles have formed patterns that are hard to break.

I still value some things that I have always tried to teach, and so I still walk a line between my previous, more "traditional" methods and my newer methods. My class is still heavily book-dependent. Most students are not reflecting directly about their own pains and oppressions. (Some are: special assignments were arranged for students from so-called Third World countries or settings.) My efforts to take praxis seriously have perhaps not yet yielded an ideal approach. In the spring I will team-teach with a black male colleague a course in which we hope to require students to do all their reflection out of their real life questions and struggles. Slowly perhaps I will move toward a more praxis-oriented approach, at least in my own small sphere. I will do what I can to change my methods of education.

But until the vision and structures of theological education change, my ability to alter my methods is limited.[45] I must still give grades, and I therefore participate in an educational system that is hierarchical, continues to be dominated by certain images of success, and carries a built-in tendency toward competition rather than cooperation. I am still responsible to an "academy" that perpetuates very traditional standards of scholarship within its own ranks.[46] I work within time constraints that often seem destructive of that humanness and "life" that oppressed people posit as the logical or rational element. I, too, live in a world where rules appear to be more important than people.[47] I look forward to a new theological seminary founded on praxis, but I suspect it will have to be the creation of another generation.[48]

Concluding Unscientific Postscript

As hinted, this essay was originally drafted in the middle of the semester. Readers will be wondering what assessment I made at the end of the semester. How did I feel about my changed course structure at the close of the experiment, and what happened to my colleague who was under review?

Let me begin with my colleague. I am happy to say that he was promoted. Perhaps especially significant is that during the review process, the faculty grappled explicitly with questions about the meaning of true scholarship. This is the good news. However, there is also bad news. Promotion did not carry tenure. Thus I suspect that the struggle is not over and that the question of scholarship will arise anew during tenure review and will present difficulties in the future as it has in the past.

As for my class: now that the semester is over I would make even more radical changes in its design and structure. To the extent possible, I would ask those from oppressed communities to come and tell their personal stories at the outset of the semester. I would ask my black colleague not to lecture on black *theology and ethics* but to talk about how his *life experiences* have affected his approach to theology and ethics. I would do the same with my colleagues from Asia and Africa. And I would risk asking those students in the class who experience everyday oppression to talk about their experiences. We would still read books from oppressed people, and we would put the more traditional academic agendas even farther back in the semester.

Whether such a redesign would be successful I do not know. It would involve some risk. For example, it is possible that the stories of my colleagues had a powerful impact on the students precisely because they came at the end of the semester in which we had worked together enough to develop some trust. Putting those stories closer to the beginning of the semester might jeopardize that trust level and result not in a commitment to the struggles of the oppressed, but in a "hardening of hearts" in which oppressors cannot hear the voices of the oppressed. Such questions represent unknowns. Every pedagogical method has its flaws, and so the experiment must continue.

6

Focusing on the Church's Mission: A Theological Inquiry

James C. Logan

The interview had proceeded extraordinarily well. Without discussion the interview committee had virtually reached its conclusion. Before us had sat for approximately two hours a most promising candidate for pastoral ministry. He had demonstrated remarkable theological astuteness, an informed and articulate mind, without "cockiness," yet nevertheless self-assured. Finally came some ecclesiology questions. He dealt with the so-called textbook questions quickly and with ease. He knew his tradition; he knew contemporary theology; he knew the church's policy and doctrinal standards. I asked him how he felt personally about the church's social creed. He quickly and, again, articulately revealed a keen social conscience. In college he had "owned" the creed, and it was one of the reasons he had decided to become an ordained minister. He was asked to apply some of the principles of the creed to what he had cited earlier as "Jesus' proclamation of the reign of God," and to show how these principles related to the person of Christ. He had no problems with this question either. Then he was asked how he saw the contemporary church, the church in which he might shortly be a pastor, translating this social witness of the church into concrete action. He stiffened but did not lose his composure. He did a concise but precise analysis of contemporary society and the complexities of its problems. He went on to indicate that he was familiar enough with social analysis to know that this extended to the institutional church as well.

This was the most insightful part of the interview. Here was a person who "had it together"! His biblical, theological, historical, ethical, psychological, homilectical, and administrative preparation had been well appropriated and assimilated. "This gives me great trouble," he confessed. "The church is not where it once was." He continued, adding almost as an afterthought, "It isn't even where it was when I entered college." He was correct.

With the growing complexity of the modern world and with our growing knowledge of this complexity, the institutional church itself is going through a rapid change. In 1920 the seven mainline denominations accounted for 76 percent of American Protestants. Since then, according to several statistical surveys, the mainliners have collectively lost more than 4,775,000 members. As a headline of *The Fundamentalist Journal* puts it, "The Mainline Is Becoming the Sideline." Religious pluralism is more obvious in our society than ever before. For example, in the United States there are more Mormons—and Muslims—than there are Episcopalians. Pentecostals match the Presbyterians in number. Roman Catholics outnumber the mainline Protestants two to one. The Protestant "establishment" has become a minority movement! "Can our church go on acting as though nothing has happened? Does it know that it has a new sociological placement in our society? How does a minority group address the major corporate issues of our time?" (He had read H.R. Niebuhr's *Christ and Culture*.)

The candidate, who was no stranger to the inside of the church, went on to observe internal conflicts, both theological and social ("Just go to an Annual Conference," he said). He sensed a growing loss of vitality of internal life (which he called spirituality) and external vision (which he called mission). Reading contemporary books about the church had not helped him much—one on the low morale of the clergy, one which claimed that the church was both locally and connectionally "out of focus," one which claimed that lay persons no longer felt called to ministry. What was even more confusing was that few analysts were able to pinpoint the "focus," and that the "out-of-focus" category was not singular, but plural. Actually the differences in analyses seemed to indicate a social picture that had fallen apart. The multiple prescriptions, frequently varying with one another, simply documented the complexity of the situation. "Has the church ever been like this before?" the candidate asked.

Descriptively the ordinand had depicted the situation of theological education today as we attempt to prepare people for effectively responsible social ministry. It is a different situation, so different that an exercise in showing the social relevance of the various doctrines of the faith is not enough, important as that, too, may be. The church is in a radically different situation, and a socially responsible ministry demands a *radical* (getting to the roots) grappling with the new situation.

Rather than "socially responsible ministry," the term mission is used. This can be misleading because rhetorically "mission" frequently replaces "missions." Mission nevertheless is used because the term embraces a wholeness of *kerygma*, *diaconia*, *koinonia*, and *martyria*. We cannot compartmentalize the church's social mission, thereby separating it from its engagement in leitourgia, evangelization, and cross-cultural witnessing. In fact all the functions so necessary to the church's calling are themselves social, and therefore cannot be artificially separated from one another. The term norm, or its adjective, normative, is used in the sense of *standard* by which we measure, as well as in the sense of *source* from which we derive, our actual *praxis*.

Mission and the Local Church

In 1984 my denomination mandated a study commission that focused on the mission to which United Methodism is called as it enters its third century of history. The Presbyterians and Lutherans have already completed similar studies for their churches. In the United Methodist study it has become evident that the future of faithful mission of the church depends on the local congregation and the leadership of its ordained ministry. Although bureaucracy may be necessary, it is not a substitute for the local church. If the church is to recover its missional impetus, the front line of that recovery will depend on the *diaconia* of the local congregation and its pastoral leadership.

This is no glib or overly optimistic observation. To be sure, there are plenty of signs of the absence of *diaconia* in the local church. Our churches have continued to engage in many valid and valuable missional activities, but they have lost the unifying vision that alone could clarify the relations among them. Local congregations have increasingly ceased to define themselves in terms of participation in a unified mission and have come more and more to see themselves as the object of the church's mission. Structures established to enable congregations to share effectively in common mission are now oriented to the service of the congregations as each determines its mission for itself.

If the need for mission to the world has declined, this turning inward of the church might be acceptable (although not by definitional standards). But the interconnected problems of widespread religious ignorance, confusion, and indifference; self-destructive habits and life-styles; violent crime; decay of the family; renewed tribalism and nationalism; hunger; environmental destruction; exhaustion of natural resources; racism; sexism; economic exploitation and decline; political oppression and war; and the threat of nuclear holocaust all call for the healing and renewing word of the gospel as never before.

In despair our culture is turning inward. Christ calls the church to new visions and new initiatives for the sake of the world God loves. This is the theological mandate that confronts us in theological education as we endeavor to prepare women and men for responsible ministry in church and society. Hand in glove with the theological responsibility is the requirement of rigorous analysis of the contemporary situation (personal, social, national, and global), if a convincing picture is to guide the church into the future.

A Case Study: "In Defense of Creation"

Perhaps a case study will help us focus. In 1986 the Council of Bishops of The United Methodist Church, after two years of careful research and theological study, sent to the local churches a pastoral epistle entitled "In Defense of Creation: The Nuclear Crisis and a Just Peace." The epistle and its supporting study document are an exercise in a "theology of *shalom*." Some of the conclusions that the bishops reached are as follows:

1. Every policy of government must be an act of justice and must be measured by its impact on the poor, the weak, and the oppressed—not only in our own nation but in all nations.
2. Security is indivisible in a world threatened with total annihilation. Unilateral security is impossible in the nuclear age.
3. All Christians, pacifists and nonpacifists alike, ought to share a strong moral presumption against violence, killing, and warfare, seeking every possible means of peaceful conflict resolution.
4. No just cause can warrant the waging of nuclear war or any use of nuclear weapons.
5. The church of Jesus Christ, in the power and unity of the Holy Spirit, is called to serve as an alternative community to an alienated and fractured world—a loving and peaceable international company of disciples transcending all governments, races, and ideologies; reaching out to all "enemies"; and ministering to all the victims of poverty and oppression.

6. Ecumenism, in all the fullness of baptism and eucharist, and in common life throughout all the earth, is the new synonym for peacemaking.

The bishops requested pastors to read the letter to their congregations and to use the foundation document that accompanied the letter for study, and sought for prayerful responses from local congregations and individuals. As of October 1986 the letter had been read in 67 percent of the churches, with another 14 percent expressing intentions to read it later in the year. The response across the church was considerably more positive than many had predicted. Understandably, negative responses generally predominated in the columns of "letters to the editor" of church-house periodicals and indicated why local congregations find difficulty in being involved in social ministry. A selection of these negative responses follows:

- Maryland (150 members): "The congregation is very suspicious of political sermons, especially if they perceive it [sic] coming from a 'liberal' perspective. I'm doing this very cautiously so as not to offend. It will take a good bit of nurture before these churches will ever embrace peace issues."
- Ohio (100 members): "These people aren't interested in world community or defense of creation—just protection of what they own or hope to own."
- Louisiana (1,000 members): "I love it. But my congregation thought the letter was urging the United States to 'throw in the towel.' "
- Illinois (160 members): "I read the letter as a servant of the bishops and not as though I approve or agree with what it said."
- Texas (3,000 members): "It would hurt the church here badly to use the pastoral letter."
- New Mexico (20 members): "I didn't read it because I and most of my congregation don't agree with it."
- Tennessee (230 members): "Until we can carry out our first responsibility, that of proclaiming the Gospel of

salvation and winning souls to Christ, I feel we have nothing to say. Further, I feel worship time is not the proper time for reading anything but the word of God."

- Ohio (1,500 members): "The document is poorly written with questionable scholarship that looks like a propaganda document. Why should we take seriously bishops who have proven themselves completely unable to move our church from death to life in their declared area of expertise, shepherding the church?"
- Indiana (120 members): "We just want to help save souls and work for the Lord in our community, so if there is nuclear war due to the nuclear weapons buildup, we will be ready to meet the Lord."

A negative response may not indicate social withdrawal, but may arise from a different theological context. Some responses were merely hesitant, while indicating openness for further study and deliberation. Some of the responses reveal the pastor's manner in handling such an issue in the congregation: one preached on the document; one chose not to read it; one kept personal distance so as not to impair personal ministry; and one read the epistle simply as an act of obedience to the bishops. Even among the positive responses (most of which belong to oral tradition) sparse are the indications of any long-range educational projections in responding to the bishops. Particular responses also give some graphic descriptions of real-life situations in the parish. Some were "very suspicious of political sermons"; some were not "interested in the world community"; some felt that priorities were out of order, that evangelism should have strong priority over social engagement. To be truthful, the responses were as pluralistic as the church is pluralistic! Yet in precisely this kind of theologically and socially pluralistic situation most of our seminarians will serve their future ministries.

An uneasiness gripped me in reading and hearing the myriad responses. Negative, ambivalent, positive—all seemed to emerge from a fragmented view of the church's engagement in mission. Whether the participants considered themselves theologically liberal or conservative, regardless of their political and social positions, they held something in common. It was as though the mission to which the church is called consisted of bits and pieces, and depending on one's predispositions, one was free to pick and choose which bit or piece one would take. "I'm not opposed to the letter," one pastor responded personally, "but this is not 'my thing.' My *forte* is pastoral care of my people." Herein lies the catch. Was mission "caring for the flock," evangelization in an increasingly neopagan society, or social engagement in the causes of justice, peace, and the physical, social, and political well-being of people? One should not have to choose. These are all urgent. What is missing, however, is a unifying vision of mission. Without a unifying vision people are left in the lurch to choose one-dimensional visions of mission. At least one denomination's experience seems to be that the vision of mission *is* fragmented and that its implementation rests on individualistic choice rather than on compelling discipleship.

A Primary Theological Reflection

Although our contemporary missional situation is one of fragmentation, our theological beginning point must be found somewhere beyond and transcending that fragmentation. In other words, merely to attempt to paste together bits and pieces, a little evangelism here supplemented with a little social engagement there, is a theologically superficial and inadequate method. We need a theologically normative vision of what the church is called to be and to do in this world in which the Creator God has placed us. A growing ecumenical and biblically grounded consensus is that mission is not derived from ecclesiology, but from *theo*-logy or the doctrine of God. This growing consensus is seen in recent ecumenical studies such as *Mission and Evangelism: An Ecumenical Affirmation.*[1] The same perspective is reflected in the mission documents of the Presbyterian Church (USA),

The Lutheran World Federation, the United Church of Christ, and the tentative draft of the United Methodist Church.

The normative missional vision begins with the affirmation that, first and foremost, mission is God's mission, the *missio Dei*. Mission begins with God, what God has done, what God is doing, and God's purposes for creation. If a unifying vision is to be recovered, it will not first be found in a so-called church's mission, but in the *missio Dei*, in the creative, redemptive, liberating, and reconciling mission of God for the sake of a sinful, broken, and suffering world.

1. In the beginning, through the divine Word, God created the heavens and the earth, and through creation and providence reigns as sovereign over all that is created. The Creator God has placed human beings in a peculiar position. Bearing the divine image, they are created for community with God and with one another and are to exercise responsibility for the care of the good creation. Because the Creator God acted out of freedom and grace, the only appropriate response to God by the human family is an equally free act of grateful obedience. The same Creator God is also the Covenant God. The Presbyterian statement succinctly expresses the unrelenting grace of God's action: "Even when the human race broke community with its Maker and with one another, God did not forsake it, but out of grace chose one family for the sake of all, to be pilgrims of promise, God's own Israel." For this reason God, with a liberating, "mighty outstretched arm," brought Israel out of oppression, in the words of the prophet Micah, to "do justice, to love mercy, and to walk humbly with God," being a living witness before the nations of the one true God and the divine intentions for creation.

2. The divine grace became human and dwelt among us as the Suffering, Serving One, Jesus Christ. In various ways he announced the consummate moment of God's mission:

The time is fulfilled, and the kingdom of God is at hand; repent, and believe in the gospel.

—Mark 1:15

The Spirit of the Lord is upon me,
because he has anointed me to preach
    good news to the poor.
He has sent me to proclaim release
    to the captives
and recovering of sight to the blind,
to set at liberty those who are oppressed,
to proclaim the acceptable year of the Lord.
                                    —Luke 4:18–19

Christ gave up equality with God and took the form of a servant. In his person, ministry, and death Jesus took on himself the alienation, sin, oppression, and injustice of a sinful age and initiated a New Divine Reign for forgiveness, righteousness, and peace for a sinfully distorted creation.

In parable, precept, and example Jesus proclaimed the New Reign of God. The Hebrew meaning of "proclamation" is the announcement of a joyous victory. Although God has reigned in creative, providential power, now, Jesus proclaims, God reigns in messianic power. For these reasons Jesus sought out the "little ones," the marginalized, "the last, the least, and the lost" who gladly heard him. By grace he extended to them the invitation to participate in God's New Reign. His mission was to inaugurate the New Reign of God definitively expressed in forgiving love, justice for the poor, redemption to new life, and reconciliation between humans and God and between brother and sister alike.

The incarnation was no ephemeral epiphany, but an earthy event, a babe born of a peasant woman, Mary. The crucifixion was no private event. It was a public execution for political reasons (otherwise, only stoning would have been required by the law). The crucifixion-resurrection unmasked the powers of this world and revealed them to be precisely what they are—the powers of God's good creation twisted and distorted into the "principalities and powers of this world," an "old age" in opposition to God's New Age.

One entered the New Age of God through the gracious call to repentance. This repentance, although deeply personal, was not individualistic. It had to do simultaneously with God and creation. It was a call to a new order of life, a new communal existence that would reflect the Creator's purposes from the beginning. Not only would the new community of disciples reflect the divine purpose, but they would also, like Jesus, their suffering, serving Lord, witness by speaking and doing what was the reality of God's New Reign. In short, they would participate in God's mission that was universal, knowing no classes, races, or conditions. They would participate in destroying the "walls of hostility" that the death of Christ had in reality abolished. A new order of relationship with God and with humankind was at hand. Person, message, death, and resurrection were fused into one indissoluble event. The witness to that event was equally indissoluble.

3. Jesus promised his disciples the Spirit, and after his crucifixion and resurrection the Spirit came upon those who waited in Jerusalem. It is impossible to locate one single "birthday" of the church. In covenant-form the church began with the call of Abraham and Sarah. In person-form the church began with Jesus Christ. Now in power-form the church begins with Pentecost. The Spirit was given not as a private possession, but as empowerment for the universal mission. By the Spirit the church was called into being as the provisional demonstration of what God intends for the whole human race. As such, the church is the "sign" of God's New Order as announced and inaugurated by the Incarnate One, Jesus. Through the Spirit the church is called to be the living reminder to the world of God's new reality, God's new creation. Through the power of the Spirit the church is called to announce to an "old age" the coming New Messianic Age and to invite people through faith and repentance into a new relationship that, through God's grace, makes all things new. Through the Spirit the church is called to participate in God's activity. Where people struggle in the bondage of sin, whether it be self-inflicted or externally imposed, the church is to announce the good news, call people to repentance and a new life. In either case the church proclaims that bondage to compulsive internal or external sin is contrary to God's will, and that liberation is at hand. It is a call to liberation both for the oppressed and the oppressor. Likewise, it is a call to

messianic discipleship participating in God's mission where wounds are to be bound up, the needs of the poor and the powerless redressed, hunger and injustice to be overcome, "sharing with Christ in the establishing of his just, peaceable, and loving rule in the world."

Without the God who creates there is no world for mission. Without a Covenant God who calls there is no imperative for mission. Without Christ there is no content and goal of mission. Without the Holy Spirit there is no power to identify with God in the *missio Dei*. The basis and unifying vision of mission lies in this triune God of grace. The church is faithful in mission when it embodies, witnesses to, and acts in conformity with the divine will.

The Contemporary Scene Revisited

The biblical sources of the Judeo-Christian tradition present a cohesive vision of mission. Individual conversion and social responsibility are a single whole. Only for purposes of analysis is it possible to separate the two. Conversion entails not just a change of mind or existential orientation. Conversion is a fundamental change in one's conduct of life. A fundamental question, nevertheless, still plagues us. How did the primal vision of God's activity and purpose become fragmented in practice? The answer to this question is multifaceted. I choose to focus on one cultural component, knowing quite well that this does not present a fully developed account. Our Western culture, including the cultural shaping of the church, is post-Enlightenment. We are creatures of the Enlightenment far more than we are creatures formed by a biblical tradition, or even the tradition of the Reformers and their children.

Lesslie Newbigin has argued this thesis with considerable cogency.[2] Newbigin is a missiologist, and in uncharacteristic fashion he has turned his attention "westward," finding in Western Christianity serious "fissures" that have resulted in a truncated gospel. Newbigin is not culturally naive. Any faith will always, in some manner, be enculturated. He does not argue for a culture-free faith, which correctly he sees to be both impossible and inadvisable. His argument is directed against an uncritical adoption of certain thought motifs of Enlightenment culture by the church.

Risking a simplistic account, some of the components of this new age must be listed if we are to comprehend the "fissures" to which Newbigin points. Newtonian science, with its strong insistence on inductive rather than deductive logic, encouraged an enthusiastic conviction that the tracing of cause-and-effect relationships in the natural world could lead to a human mastery over that world. Already Descartes had set the stage by making the distinction between a subjective thinking self and an objective, extended world of matter. Human reason moved more and more from the deductive and speculative metaphysics of former times to a mathematical and analytical definition reflected in Kant's two critiques, one of theoretical and one of practical reason. "Knowledge" took on a new definition. Knowledge consisted of the factually describable, while moral and religious judgments were consigned to the status of postulates.

In the areas of political and economic thought emphasis fell on human rights to life, liberty, and property. The divine right of kings was shifting to the inalienable rights of individuals. The Enlightenment was the age of reason; it was the age of individual rights; it was the age of government "from below" rather than "from above." The list of historical changes could be extended, but these will suffice to indicate the dawn of a new age. Knowledge consisted of facts, and it was always individual reason that discovered the facts. Rights were individual rights, and government by contract existed to ensure those rights, particularly the right to property. Reason, knowledge, rights—these rested on the individual "thinking things out from below" (Kant).

Few thinking Westerners today will quibble about the giant steps taken in the physical sciences. Scarce would be the number of those who would opt to return to a prescientific, predemocratic society. Philosophically and theologically some may question the advisability of splitting reason between the theoretical and the practical, and hence jettisoning the metaphysical enterprise. But no philosopher or theologian can today define reason for methodological purposes without taking into account the Kantian "Copernican" revolution. And although one may justly critique the utopian optimism found in the heavenly city of the eighteenth-century philosophers, few would fault, at least in principle, the focus on the rights of individual people.

In the next two centuries Protestantism accommodated its thought to the main currents of the Enlightenment. When the conservative theologians were pressed to defend their propositional truths under pressure from the new critical "enlightenment," they tended to move themselves into the very arena of the Enlightenment by developing apologetics ("evidences") that depended on the Enlightenment's own demands for factual evidence and rational—if not rationalistic—proof of the theological propositions. Liberal theologians at the other end of the spectrum tended to adopt the social, humanistic values of the Enlightenment and press the theological tradition (even change the tradition) to support these values. After all, they were the "values of Jesus." This, no doubt, is the reason conservative and liberal theological parties are so effective in their infrastructural warfares in the church. They are both children of the Enlightenment, roughly taking their positions on one end or the other of the Enlightenment spectrum while savoring the Enlightenment food more than either suspects.

Behind and within the more obvious developments of the Enlightenment lie some ideational configurations that are still components of the thought structures of most Western Christians whether they are conscious of such or not, be they conservative or liberal. These ideational configurations play themselves out as Newbigin's "fissures," and they are still very much alive in the thought of many Christians whether in pew or pulpit. I point to only three of these "fissures" because I believe them to be pivotal to understanding intellectually and conceptually the debate about mission in the contemporary church.

1. *The "fissure" between "fact" and "value."* For the Enlightenment mind, fact consisted of that which was self-evidently

true; or of much greater import, fact was that which could be scientifically (cause and effect) proved whether one was dealing with material reality or historical reality. Kant's "starry heavens above and the moral law within" is the dictum and classic illustration of the Enlightenment's definition of "fact." Scientifically fact was that which could be subjected to cause-effect scrutiny and thereby ascertained as valid or invalid. Was this not Kant's attempt when he wrote *Religion Within the Limits of Reason Alone?* Teleology or purposiveness had intentionally been eliminated from the definition of fact. The intellectual concern was to demonstrate what *is*, and no logical connection seemed to exist between *is* and *ought*. Humans, however, are value-making and value-living creatures. Value for the Enlightenment mind depended on subjective choice determined either by inference from "fact" (hence, a postulate) or by some innate "feeling" that could not be subjected to scientific investigation or proof.

2. *The "fissure" between "objective" and "subjective."* Closely paralleling the "fissure" between "fact" and "value" was the contrast between "objective" and "subjective." The same rules held. That which is objectively real is that which can be subjected to empirical, rational proof. Like "value," the "subjective" was consigned to the status of the innate, intuitive, or "feeling." As the Enlightenment progressed, religion came more and more to be viewed as "value," and hence as "subjective," as contrasted with demonstrable "fact." This development presented serious consequences for the church's involvement in the public arena. And this leads to the third paralleling "fissure."

3. *The "fissure" between "public" and "private."* For the Enlightenment mind, the "public" arena was controlled by rational, scientific analysis and prescription. Sociologically and politically the church of Christendom had been dethroned. In the medieval city the streets radiated from the hub, which was the city square on which the church or cathedral was situated. The church was at the center of the public arena. In the Enlightenment the church was shifted to a side street. Belonging to the church was no longer a primary socially

necessitous decision; it was a secondary optional decision. Its ministry was essentially to the private needs of individuals. When Jurgen Moltmann critiques the churches' retreat to ministries to isolated "islands of meaning," he attributes this to a capitulation of the church to technological societal developments. After all, technological society is an extension, although in many respects radically different, of Enlightenment, industrial society.

The Enlightenment "fissure" between the "public" and the "private" buttressed by the "fissures" of "fact" and "value," "objective" and "subjective" are still in the minds of many of us. "We just want to help save souls and work for the Lord in our community, so if there is nuclear war due to the nuclear weapons buildup, we will be ready to meet the Lord." How often the pastor is confronted with variations on this statement! A bifurcated, if not fragmented, missional vision arises in great part from the still much alive "fissures" of our Enlightenment tradition.

The Missional Norm Revisited

Well known is the fact that the great progenitor of liberal Protestantism Friedrich Schleiermacher decidedly placed theology on one side of the Enlightenment "fissures." Revivalism, with no recognition of any similarity with liberal theological thought, did much the same thing in the nineteenth century in the United States by translating the great Reformation doctrines of justification and sanctification into subjective experiential terms. To be sure, the Evangelical Awakening, as early as John Wesley in the eighteenth century and exemplified by some of the leading figures of nineteenth-century revivalism in the United States, sought to reconcile the "fissures" by insisting that "new birth" and sanctification led to the sanctification of society itself. Dwight L. Moody, however, could say, "God has placed me in a raft on a stormy sea and said, 'Moody, save as many drowning souls as possible.'" Individualism was, however, such a dominant factor in the social fabric that the revivalistic movement played a leading role in the continuation of the eighteenth- and nineteenth-century "fissures." To return to academic theology, strange as it may sound, such a leading twentieth-century theologian as Rudolf Bultmann played a role in developments in this direction also. The Bultmannian program of hermeneutical demythologization, with its sharp distinctions between *Historie* and *Geschichte* ("fact" and "value") effectively removes the church and the gospel from the "public" arena and confines them to individual existence, thereby privatizing ministry to individual "self-understanding."

This is not to disparage the attempt of Schleiermacher to address in the name of the Christian faith "the cultured despisers of religion" of his day or ours. Nor should we belittle the tremendous efforts and considerable success of the nineteenth-century revivalists to call an ethically rough and tumble culture to the saving grace of Christ often accompanied with remarkably ethical consequences in the lives of repentant men and women. Certainly Bultmann was theologically correct in insisting on the basis of the Pauline doctrine of justification by grace through faith that we are not saved by "facts" (as defined by the Enlightenment).

The fundamental issue for the theologian-pastor is, How in the name of Christ do we as Christians address society? The return to Christendom in which the church had a definite "public" role in society is not an option, nor should it be. Yet our fundamental theological responsibility in equipping people for a socially responsible ministry is to call into question some of the fundamental assumptions of a post-Enlightenment culture, assumptions that may in reality be illusions.

We have seen in the missional norm discussed earlier that the biblical understanding of the *missio Dei* does not manifest the "fissures" of "fact" and "value," of "objective" and "subjective," of "public" and "private." Creation is a worldly event, and the divine reign over the creation knows of no compartments or arenas of worldly life that are exempt from that sovereign reign of God. The call of a covenant people was not for special privilege, but for special responsibility—

to be "a light unto the nations." God's election of a particular people is carried forth with the divine "eye" on the nations. Under the covenant no separation exists between piety and public action. Covenant people qua covenant people do justice, love mercy, and walk humbly with their God.

From Bethlehem to Calvary the ministry of Jesus was in public view and was for the public. His proclamation of God's New Time, as in Israel, knew no enclaves hidden or isolated from divine judgment and divine redemption. No event could have been more public and decisive for the public than the crucifixion. Pilate may be the pathetic political pawn, but Christ disarms the powers of this world—be they political, economic, or social—of their distortion, pretension, and oppression. Indeed, so extensive is the nexus of crucifixion-resurrection that the authors of the letters to the Ephesians and Colossians witness to it as a cosmic event. And although the call to Christ and his messianic discipleship is deeply personal, it is not individualistic. It is not "value" as contrasted with "fact"; it is not "subjective" as contrasted with "objective"; it is not "private" as contrasted with "public." In fact, it is the event that transcends these polarities and reveals them for what they are: purely human constructs that for the Christian are subject to the critical scrutiny of Christ and his disciples. It is a call under the cross to a life of discipleship in which one lives and dies, not caught between humanly constructed polarities, but for the world for which Christ lived and died.

The early church could have had it otherwise. They could have taken their place among cults of the empire. These cults promised private and individual meaning but did not challenge the political power of Caesar. To the contrary, the early church quite consciously placed itself in the open public when it boldly proclaimed, "Jesus is Lord." The message was simultaneously a theological affirmation and a political confrontation. If the reality of Christ had been "subjective" and "private," the church would have been a private cult, and members would not have experienced persecution and martyrdom. Yet to have taken the route of the private cult would have been a blatant denial of the universal mission to which they had been called. It would have also been a denial of the Great Commission under which they lived and died: "All authority in heaven and on earth has been given to me. *Go* therefore and *make* disciples of all nations, *baptizing* them. . . , *teaching* them to *observe* all that I have *commanded* you [Matt. 28:18–20, italics added]." Celsus and other writers applied to the religious societies the Greek terms *thiasos* and *hieranos*, which underscored their privacy and separation from any political connotations. The Christians quite consciously appropriated the vernacular word *ecclesia*, which meant a public gathering, more than likely in the marketplace. They called themselves the *ecclesia tou theou*. Apparently they clearly wanted to be known as the "public assembly of God." A public cross, a public assembly under the cross—these are the reasons they were willing to pay the price.

An Ecclesial Proposal

Certainly systematic theology as a discipline has a responsibility to interpret doctrine as integrally one in its personal (as contrasted with individualistic) and social dimensions. The missional norm, stated earlier, implies and requires a systematic presentation of a theology of creation, covenant, the incarnate and redeeming Christ, mission, church, and eschatology. Doing a systematic theological treatment of this missional story, however, lies beyond the scope of this essay. To use a traditional term, the concern here is with *prolegomenon*.

Theology has a prolegomenous task working conjointly with other disciplines in critically examining our cultural context and content. Because culture itself is never static (or else it dies), theology must be an ongoing effort on the part of the church to "give reasons for the hope within us" in whatever cultural setting we find ourselves. This will, of necessity, entail a certain cultural translation. Such cultural translation must, however, be done *critically*. Theology's prolegomenous task is one of cultural critique particularly pertaining to theology's own enculturation. We must critique the conceptual language that we use because that very language shapes Christian perception.

Newbigin, in his analysis, concludes that "Christians will have to learn that conversion is a matter not only of the heart and the will but also of the mind."[3] What is troublesome with this conclusion is that we still have distinctions or functions, although not quite "fissures," of "heart," "will," and "mind," without integral unity. Certainly Newbigin does not intend these to be construed as Platonic distinctions. Earlier he argues for a unitary view of the human. What is missing in his argument, however, is a consideration of the church as the context of conversion. It is within ecclesial community that "heart," "will," and "mind" become one. What, therefore, is needed is an *ecclesial conversion.* This is difficult for Westerners, particularly Christians in the United States, to perceive. We have drunk of the wine of individualism, volunteerism, and self-realization to the extent that little ecclesial consciousness is left to draw on. Seventy-five years ago the British Congregationalist theologian Peter Taylor Forsyth[4] lamented that most church members saw their collectivity as a beautiful arrangement of individually cut flowers. Conversion of "heart," "will," and "mind" remain ambiguously related without a genuine ecclesial conversion. Further yet, the church is not only the context of conversion; it is itself the communal substance of conversion. One is converted not only to a new relationship with God and others, nor only to a new perspective that intellectually transcends the Enlightenment "fissures," but one is converted to the missional God to live as an integral part of the missionary body of Christ. Conversion of mind is vitally important, but without a community that forms and reforms, the conversion is short-lived. Christian community, ecclesial reality, is what fuses justification and sanctification into a unified whole—faith active in love.

What, then, is ecclesial reality? The church is characterized by a peculiar form of discourse. The church is a story-shaped community. George A. Lindbeck has recently reminded us that being and growing as a Christian is like learning a language.[5] When the language is properly understood, it shapes a new world of reality. So it is with the church. It is not the church that creates mission; to the contrary it is the story of the missional God that forms and shapes the church. Theologically speaking, the *missio Dei* precedes church and gives birth to the church. This is not to say that the church *is mission*. The church is the doxological community that exists by grace through *kerygma, koinonia, martyria,* and *diaconia* to render its praise to the coming and sending God. Doxology, no matter what form it takes, is not empty language. Be it creed, hymn, prayer, or whatever, it is formative language. In Lindbeck's terms, such language creates a new reality—ecclesial reality. Because such language is not empty, the church lives its life in mission because its formative story is the missional story of God and creation and sin and redemption and liberation. Mission is not some optional activity of the church, but a fundamental ecclesial mark of its identity.

Living in a society whose language and values are frequently at variance with the missional story of creation, covenant, Christ, church, and consummation, the church cannot depend on the larger society to convey the story; nor can the church accept society's definition and consignment of its ecclesial being. Therefore a primary task of the church in fulfilling its calling to mission is simply, although it is not a simple matter, to form Christians. Such formation of necessity involves the church in a radical critique of society. The church primarily does this, as William H. Willimon states,[6] by "detoxifying" its participants of the lethal, toxic "chemicals" that infest the lives of modern men and women. This task has to be performed again and again because Christians are not so much born as formed. The "detoxification" is only the beginning. Being formed by a story that is at variance with society's story is an intentional, continual process. Churches that have been active in social reform have usually "laid upon the society" social and ethical directives that the church has frequently been powerless to form in its own body. In turn when the socially active church addresses itself, more frequently it speaks *to* the church than *out* of the church.

Israel, at its high moments, was a people formed by the

covenant story. When the memory of the story faded, they succumbed to the idea that they possessed a story (hence a favored people) rather than to the idea that they were a story-formed people who were claimed and possessed by the story. The prophets rise to call the people back to the formative story of the covenant. The same is true for the Christian church. The church does not have a story, but is formed by the story. When this is forgotten the vision of being the church under the cross in and for the world pales and petrifies, or fragments and falls apart. Ecclesiologically and logically, this is to say that *being* and *doing* are sequentially ordered. We "be" as we "do."

The church is not only to *be*, but also to *be sent*. The missional story inseparably links the verbs *be* and *sent*. Without the *being*, any involvement in the world is vacuous of healing meaning. Without the *sending*, the church can easily find additional reasons for becoming more self-centered and self-serving than it already is. Bonhoeffer and others of the Confessing Church through travail and agony found this truth—being and acting are inseparable. They are inseparable because the ex-centric God seen in Jesus Christ forms an ex-centric people.

An ethics of formation is logically primary, but in no sense is it in tension with an ethics of command and action. In fact, in being is the command heard. Hearing without being/doing is apostasy. In fact, if we are not careful, we may add another "fissure" to our post-Enlightenment culture: the translated "fissure" of "hearing" (subjective) and "doing" (objective). In fact, the disciples of Christ are both "the salt [an Old Testament metaphor for covenant] of the earth" and the "light of the world." The church cannot be one without the other.

Conclusions

From this analysis a plethora of conclusions could be drawn relating to the teaching of systematic theology in the seminary's curriculum. Certainly systematic theology cannot be approached as a discrete discipline in itself. Indeed it would be difficult to defend systematic theology and Christian social ethics as independent disciplines. If thinking and being and doing are inextricably one, there is faithful theology that is not socially responsible. Likewise, systematic theology cannot be studied as though it existed in a cultural vacuum. Systematic theology is a culturally critical discipline, or else it fails to be theologically responsible.

The most important conclusion, however, has to do with community life of the seminary. If the church is a story-shaped community, nowhere is that story made more explicit than in corporate worship. Certainly worship is not a means to an end. Liturgy is the rendering unto the missional God the totality of our missional response as an offering of "our souls and bodies." In the ecclesial reality of the worshiping community we see something of the wholeness of faithful discipleship. While the seminary is not the church, it is nevertheless the "seed-bed" (seminal) of the church's ministerial leadership. Communal worship is therefore not an option among options. Communal worship is the fundamental context in which everything else the seminary endeavors to do holds together.

7

Learning with the Justice-active Church
Public Ministry in Ecclesial Context

Dieter T. Hessel

This chapter is not another exercise in seminary-bashing, but an attempt to discern the ecclesial pattern of vigorous public ministry, and to suggest implications for theological education in the 1990s. I leapfrog the standard complaint that theological academies need to "pay more attention to ordinary parish reality and to train clergy accordingly." Rather than try to close that perennial gap or to gauge how much "readiness" for the average congregation the seminary fosters, I focus on qualities of the eco-justice church that deserve attention in any reform of theological education.

The seminary community, being a school of the church, is mandated to respond to it. But to which church, doing what? Much that happens in M.Div. and D.Min. study already seems to be alert to realities of the typical congregation and relevant to the preparation of parish clergy for roles as chaplain-managers of a timid church adapted to decaying culture.

106

In contrast, theological education concerned with responsible leadership for public ministry will develop pastors who refuse merely to accommodate to culture and class, or to confine their service to "sheep already in the fold."

My thesis is that the task of theological education for social ministry comes into view as we live with, take part in, and study justice-oriented-and-active congregations (JOACS). Their dynamics are illustrated by five groups of rather daring parish churches I have encountered in my work. These justice-active congregations focus on one or more of the following concerns: Public Sanctuary, More Light Ministry (regarding sexual orientation), Life-style Change, Poverty-Impacted Community Survival, or Ecumenical Solidarity (peacemaking) across ideological lines. Taken together, these socially engaged congregations witness to economic and ecological justice, racial-gender-age inclusiveness, community rebuilding, and pursuit of peace. A focus on their quality ecclesial praxis helps to clarify some priorities for theological educators. By examining distinctive habits or qualities of these mainstream Protestant congregations (and related missionary structures) that do social ministry, plus the dilemmas they experience in this public witness, we can pinpoint a whole conception and several competencies that seminarians—on the way to becoming faithful, effective, professional or volunteer parish leaders—"most need to learn to equip them" for public ministry (stated symposium purpose #2, noted in the Preface). In short, education for public ministry will be revitalized to the extent that seminary and eco-justice church join, and critically reflect, on common pilgrimage toward new humanity in a crowded world.[1]

What moves congregations to undertake and stay engaged in eco-justice ministry—to work for structural change or social transformation even as they share with other congregations such standard habits as worshiping together, caring for one another, nuturing the young, and showing compassion for society's victims? The composite sketch begun below that others can fill in is based on years of pondering what justice-active congregations do, and how they are led to do it.[2] Much that I have learned on the subject comes from time spent—often as a member of a visiting team—in leadership development with parish and regional church leaders who want to minister in ways that meet the demands of a rapidly approaching eco-justice future. Congregations of all sizes—these observations are scale-neutral—become justice active or develop shalom ministry to the extent that they do the following things imaginatively in combination (there being no substitute for imagination and wholism anywhere in ecclesial life; we are dealing more with developing an art form than with applying a science):

1. *Justice-active congregations meet and minister with others, particularly the oppressed, and reposition the church to walk in solidarity with powerless people.*

Congregations that are open to or directly exposed to strangers—that is, strikingly different people or deprived groups—are most likely to become justice-oriented and active. It is quite apparent that no amount of Bible study or personal faith testimony will substitute for rubbing shoulders with the *anawim*—whom the Hebrew Penteteuch, Psalms, and Prophets refer to as the poor, marginated, dispossessed, or powerless whose liberation God promises through the establishment of just relationships. As oppressed people or brutalized nature and its spokespersons encounter us, opening our eyes to a particular "view from below," we experience a quickening of a common passion for justice (or a passionate sense of injustice) and insist that the disregarded be treated with the same dignity we want for ourselves.

This is not to say that exposure to injustice and dire human need automatically leads to socially repositioning results. Exposure to "others" may only increase natural tendencies to withdraw into familiar enclaves of homogenous community and to make apartheid arrangements that insulate ourselves from difficulties of social pluralism or transforming action. (The Pharisees are paradigmatic of the hands-off response that tempts every congregation and generation of believers.) Yet, in the words of Jorge Lara-Braud, "a homogenous church in a heterogenous world is an ecclesiastical heresy."

108

So the Spirit has to intercede to foster a hospitable, inclusive church in which strangers are reconciled and God's people are liberated from prisons of ideology or convention.

As stated in the 1983 Ecumenical Affirmation on Mission and Evangelism, "there is no evangelism without solidarity; there is no Christian solidarity that does not point toward the promises of the Kingdom of God." Social *repositioning* begins through encountering disadvantaged strangers, attending to the view from below, moving to repent of injustice, and reflecting on each phase of this experience in light of the living Word of God. Result: the *anawim* are understood to be an indispensable part of the church—guides to and coequal members in ministry. With their prophetic help as people with insight gained "on the margin," congregations can become engaged with current "problems and crises *through* which God calls the church to act. The church, guided by the Spirit, humbled by its own complicity and instructed by attainable knowledge, seeks to discern the will of God and learn how to obey in these concrete situations." (Confession of 1967, #42)

2. *Justice-active congregations offer critical social analysis to make the EEC connections, attending carefully to the view from below.*

About what? Critical social analysis today attempts to look trifocally at economic, ecological, and community dimensions of public problems. (These are not separate kinds of issues, but linked facets of eco-justice concern.) Few congregations (or church agencies and theologians) have as yet comprehended the full EEC links in the "eco-justice" agenda—combining justice to people with justice to the rest of creation[3]—that the near future demands. But they are moving in this direction. As William Gibson said at a December 1986 national ecumenical gathering, "love of earth and people—seeking common well-being on a thriving planet—is the unified eco-justice agenda because earth and people are one creation . . . [whose] claim to be loved is surely the Creator's claim."

On approaching the 1990s the "Justice Church" portrayed

by Fred Herzog (1980) is becoming an eco-justice church with an enriched view from below that encompasses class, race, sex, and the rest of creation. Because this church views the world as God's public household, it is more aware of a threatening arms race and widening rich/poor gap, with widespread job-skidding and impoverishing economic development, overlaid by the cruel dynamics of racism, militarism, and patriarchy. It also comprehends destruction of communities along with rapid depletion of high-quality resources—both renewable and nonrenewable. The eco-justice church would defend creation by challenging obsolete socio-economic assumptions, discerning "forced options" ahead, resisting known injustices, and acting coalitionally for a sustainable sufficiency that benefits all. This remains a difficult task because there is so much to discern and critical social consciousness still tends to be fragmentary. For example, advocates of ecological protection may not see distributive justice impacts. Disregard for working class or poor people on the part of ecologists often mirrors lack of ecological sensitivity among community action leaders who seek more jobs and neighborhood human services.

In June 1985, at a gathering to explore the prospects for a conference on Christianity and ecology, I found myself in conversation with an Arizona rancher-attorney who does quasi-organic farming near the Mexican border. His first reaction on learning of my Presbyterian national staff role was point blank surprise. "I never met a Presbyterian who wasn't a developmentalist." Fair enough. The mainstream churches have been almost as slow as the Fundamentalists to recognize the rights of creation. Later we traded options about the Sanctuary Trial verdicts. When I shared my strong convictions about the necessity for public sanctuary and indicated my personal engagement in this ministry, he became quite impatient, saying, "I can't support sanctuary because it lets people stay here who just increase ecological destruction. More than ever, we need ZPG [zero population growth], so I'm for closing the border, except for 'wetbacks' we have to use on the ranches." Then a smile crossed his face as we both recognized contradictions in which we are caught and the

110

complexity of working for a humane, sustainable future. These times challenge all of us to grasp the perspective and practice of eco-justice.

Critical social analysis that would orient church members to Justice, Peace, and the Integrity of Creation (JPIC—in WCC Vancouver Assembly terms) fosters methods of discernment that move from personal storytelling, to disciplined marshaling of social policy facts, to examining underlying dynamics and roots of eco-injustice, seeking clarity about operative ethical norms and needed directions for reform. Participants in this reflective process or spiral begin to shed the cocoon of conventional culture, recognize historical blind spots, articulate alternatives to the controlling ideology, and see the direction for constructive social policy change.

From where. Leaders of justice-active congregations tend to be self-aware of the limitations of their social location in a particular class, gender, race, culture, and environment. So their approach to social analysis-ethics-education pays special attention to powerless groups and groaning creation. It recognizes that what we see in social analysis depends on where we stand and with whom we stand. It assumes that those who are in power have some but not most of the expertise to inform their use of excess power. People who are most vulnerable to existing policies or are working to change policy on behalf of the powerless and to include the disregarded in social policy decision-making have special expertise to guide our justice-action.

Because our social and environmental location tends to alienate us from powerless people and disregarded creatures, our method of social analysis needs to consult four kinds of "experts": (1) the vulnerable population or victims of a given policy; (2) agents of change who lead voluntary organizations, seeking constructive reforms of policy for the sake of low-power people and the habitat; (3) established powers in public office and managers of corporate entities who are responsible for administering current policy; and (4) independent students of major public issues, including scholars and journalists, whose analysis is not part of a contracted service to the powers. I have already noted the crucial role of the first and second set of experts in pushing any congregation to reposition itself. Yet justice-active congregations also need to use their access to holders of political-economic power and people in the knowledge-information industry. Adequate social analysis, therefore, also entails consulting with the third and fourth sets of experts about feasible policy reforms to redistribute power and resources.

Given the situation of most parish leaders as *both/and* people—beneficiaries of existing power arrangements who want to be with and for the oppressed—the church's special role is to facilitate a repositioning choice by adherents. Although no one can choose a different social location, one can choose social position—whose side to be on—in the struggle for JPIC. Moreover if God gives preferential option to and is heard anew among the oppressed, and if choosing to be with the oppressed is the path to our own deliverance from bondage, then the real saving option is not whether, but how to demonstrate such commitment.

3. *Justice-active congregations express theological clarity about the ecclesial and social implications of God's loving justice.*

Repositioning occurs and is sustained as church leaders creatively show that life with others is a sign that Christ continues to "bring the far off near" and to "break down the walls of hostility" between race, sex, class, culture, or nation, drawing us who have been far off from the powerless into a new life of service with the advocacy for the oppressed. JOACS concentrate on developing a disciplined although different liturgy, ethic, and style that witnesses to the loving justice of God. They explore and help adherents to grasp a spirited theological vision of shalom and the covenant purpose of history. Their biblical interpretation and theological reflection offer a moral-social vision informed by scripture and tradition as well as experience.

A theology and ethic of JIPC is understood to be distinctive of the people of God, body of Christ, and community of the Spirit. It is an "onlook toward praxis" or a way of being consistent with the main theme of the biblical story and its embodiment in the heritage and future of social mission.

Preaching in justice-active congregations tends to emphasize that passion for justice is coequal with, even prior to, compassionate service. As the "kingdom of God" shapes right relationships—restoring shalom—the realm of justice relations cannot be narrowed to the confines of voluntarism and individualism. Therefore, preachers in these congregations offer a critique of potent God concepts that misshape community and economic life.

Justice-active congregations tell a socially lively story, often sharing a "lore" that summarizes their usable history and communal wisdom. This lore, observes pastor-consultant George Wilson, is often associated with events in the community's life—adventures, crises, cherished memories. Development of a social ministry lore—communicated in performing arts, shared songs and observances, as well as special study—signifies that a congregation believes that it has something important to pass on. Its story communicates a willingness to be different from "gentile" churches and an intention to push the larger church to witness to the New Reformation.

4. *Justice-active congregations educate their members by and for mission.*

These congregations recognize that learning occurs in a continuous action/reflection process, and that the church educates by engaging in CM_2 (common ministry and current mission). To put the matter in a memorable formula, Education or $E = CM_2$. It is not a matter of first studying the Bible or theology and then figuring out how to apply an instructed faith in mission/ministry. Involvement in common ministry and current mission impinges on theological study interactively, rather than consequentially. Moreover a major purpose of biblical-theological study is to reflect on the common ministry and current mission to which God calls us, and therefore to probe and discuss our faith in proximity to our actual engagement in CM_2. In short, *conscientious reflective practice* is the educative matrix for faith formation and authentic theological maturing.

An orientation to education by and for mission leads socially engaged parish churches to cultivate several habits: (a) They mesh intentional study/discussion with mission priorities and worship life. They appreciate that what goes on in liturgy and education deeply affects the congregations' justice orientation.

(b) They select a few public issues to explore well, with every intention to act on them. This breaks the cycle of Sunday morning "Rotary Club" programming and reinforces the action/reflection style wherein groups take time to learn what they really need to know to join in significant action for justice and peace. Much of this study takes place in the midst of committee or task force work.

(c) Justice-active congregations can study controversial subjects freely. Their members expect to air hot issues and hear strongly held viewpoints from leaders and members alike, without worrying too much about disagreement on the way to set policies. They value exploring and meeting urgent issues as a way to evangelize (as many of them were evangelized).

5. *Justice-active congregations foster E-J values in their institutional life and in their work of social service/reform/resistance.*

The apostle Paul urged: "Do not be conformed to this world but be transformed by the renewal of your mind. . . . Let your manner of life be worthy of the gospel [Rom. 12:2; Phil. 1:27]."

In their life together and in their public witness these congregations affirm (a) the communal nature of human existence and (b) the socially transforming role of the faith community.

a. Congregational life together for the sake of shalom has emerged as an "organic" growth factor (distinct from numerical growth) for North American Christian communities adapting the base-community model to voluntary religious organizations in a pluralistic society. The objective is to care for one another while seeking economic/environmental justice and rebuilding community. Organic growth has a lot to do with the gerunds of ecclesial life together: worshiping, consuming, eating, offering, giving, sharing, playing, celebrating, learning, advocating, empowering.[4]

b. The congregation or one of its subgroups develops a healthy life not by seeking to become a separate beloved community, but by facing outward and participating in the public household. A congregation fosters Eco-Justice values as members attend to social needs-issues-policies, care for victims, take part in ethical discourse, and act as leaven for empowerment and transformation.

Transforming social ministry spans the continuum of service-reform-resistance and tries not to be preoccupied with any one of them. On this continuum of responses to public issues the church works to compensate for, to protest, to change, or to overcome unjust social policy.[5] Socially engaged congregations, recognizing that there are plural ways to act for shalom, tend to use the full continuum of responses both simultaneously and sequentially in their social mission engagement. Sanctuary ministry provides a current example. It began *sequentially* by first helping the refugees in their immediate need for shelter, food, and medical and legal aid; then trying to reform the Immigration and Naturalization Service (INS) practice by calling for just application of the 1980 Refugee Act to Central Americans fleeing civil war; and then defying the government's attempt to send refugees back to persecution and death. But the strategies continue to be pursued *simultaneously*. While protecting and even hiding refugees we are simultaneously advocating congressional action to force Justice Department observance of the human rights of political refugees from Central America. And although we defy the INS, we still appeal to it to humanize, depoliticize, and regularize its procedures.

The illustration also exposes another basic habit of publicly engaged parishes—they act for social change by supporting local community organizing and joining public policy advocacy networks.

6. *Justice-active congregations develop a qualitative, whole approach to public ministry that encompasses all the modes of parish life.*

A lively congregation becomes a faithful, witnessing community through multiple modes of ministry developed in creative combination with theological depth and concentraled focus (detailed in my book *Social Ministry*[6]). Basic modes of social ministry include:

- Resocialized liturgy, prayer, and proclamation
- Communal Bible study and other parish education
- Pastoral care to empower lay ministry

- Renewal of community ministry through social service and community organization/development
- Church involvement in public policy advocacy
- Institutional governance/corporate responsibility

The first group of three modes (above the line) has seldom been perceived as social ministry. The second group of three modes has seldom been developed in regular congregational life. The first set of modes needs to be resocialized beyond the private and psychological dimensions that have so preoccupied parish pastors and officers. The second set of modes can be reappropriated as "real stuff" for parish ministry along with the first set, and not merely as optional for those congregations that have time or inclination. Justice-active congregations tend to use the modes as a set in response to each major social concern. Activity occurs in several above- and below-the-line modes together, although there may be concentration on only a few of them at a time.

Consider, for example, the relationship between two of the modes: public policy advocacy and pastoral care to empower lay ministry. Personal troubles often are rooted in public policies, or lack of them. Leaders of justice-active congregations take local-regional-national politics seriously, and expect that public affairs issues and the viewpoints of various candidates for public office will be discussed by the church as a facet of its community service and public policy advocacy. Such congregations also tend to maintain nonpartisan dialogue with public officials about the values at stake in social policy choices. Still daily work is as important as public policy to the ministry of social change. So these congregations also identify and use special skills of their members for ministry-on-the-job and ministry-through-church groups to serve JPIC values.

7. A justice-active congregation usually majors in one priority social mission concern and one significant community-building initiative.

Congregations that sustain a ministry of social engagement do not just dabble in occasional study of "social issues." Each congregation tends to concentrate for years on a couple of major concerns—usually on one large global concern and an important local community need. Some local churches are still tempted to take a scatter-shot approach to a lot of issues, but most socially engaged parishes do focus. They major in a priority social mission concern consistent with current denominational (or regional ecumenical) social policy emphases. Even then, some JOACS may try to choose between being either global or local, losing touch with geographic parish responsibilities on the one hand, or becoming too parochial on the other. But the better led ones carefully do both, periodically highlighting the connections in their mission statement, public worship, stewardship education, deployment of members and funds.

The objective is not to be local or global, but to be both in a focused manner. Because these congregations focus their social concern and action, using all the modes of ministry and enlisting the special talents of individuals (members and nonmembers alike), they are able to make a public difference or to "occupy public space" (Bonhoeffer).

8. Justice-active congregations use connectional resources (denominational, ecumenical, and coalitional) for cosmopolitan ministry.

No congregation does significant social ministry by going it alone, no matter how residentially based (which some aren't). Congregations are strengthened in social witness and ministry as their leaders and members link their mission strategy with regional and denominationwide agencies, with ecumenical councils and clusters of churches, with community organizations and specialized training centers, and with coalitional interfaith groups. To do this effectively requires both self-confidence and graceful patience. Justice-active churches find themselves to be midwives of social invention in situations where accountability and consensus are typically not clear. In ecumenical-coalitional work concerned with community organization and public policy advocacy usually no one is in charge. Yet signs of movement toward human unity are to be found in maturing ecumenical movement by congregations and larger church bodies "open to opportunities for conversation, cooperation and action [for JPIC] with other ecclesiastical bodies and secular groups" (PCUSA Form of Government, Ch. 15). Socially engaged congregations often provide local leadership in ecumenical and coalitional work.

As for relationships within the denomination, such congregations often remain uneasy about the larger ecclesiastical system, making full use of its resources, including denominational social policy reports, program specialists, and funds. But they don't expect much support when controversy intensifies. The plain fact is that justice-active congregations usually are ahead, and may have to disregard certain rules, of their own denomination to undertake a significant social witness. Yet this self-sufficiency does not seem to hinder the ability of these congregations to make alliances and join coalitions where there are common interests. Perhaps the secret to this approach is its recognition that creativity requires some marginality from conventional institutional religion on the one hand, while developing partnerships with responsible groups and ecclesiastical structures on the other hand.

This often leads a socially engaged congregation to open its buildings(s) to a variety of community uses and groups—some unconventional—and to make creative use of financial assets in community development or for other service-and-justice initiatives.

9. *Justice-active congregations usually model a mutual-ministry reconception of member, officer, and clergy roles.*Emphasis is on empowering the laity to make use of their gifts for *ministry in, as,* and *through* the church (Cameron Hall), while humanizing the clergy to be vulnerable and engaged as leading partners in common ministry. Several important shifts of

congregational life-style are involved. Most important, the congregation understands itself to be a faith community that is undergoing change while sharing responsibility to carry out daily ministry in scattered locations. Mutuality gradually displaces hierarchy. Shared expertise and responsibility reduce zigzagging when incumbent pastors leave. The congregation makes better use of the pastor's special talents (obviously, they need justice-oriented and active pastors!), while it tries not to become dependent on clergy for mission direction. New officers are oriented toward, and leaders developed to serve, the church's purpose and JPIC concerns.

There are obvious implications of this style shift for the way pastor(s) function in partnership with lay leaders and how the congregation's officers behave—not as a board of directors with an executive chief above the fray. They all lead in the actual doing of social ministry. In leadership style, socially engaged congregations also attend to dynamics of voluntary organizational development (O.D.), affirming the axiom that O.D. does not generate social ministry, but congregational social ministry goes awry or withers whenever leaders ignore voluntary organization realities. Justice-active congregations try to hear concerns and ideas of members, remove blocks to communication where known, confront important issues directly with procedural patience, and grant initiating groups or committees plenty of latitude to implement a discernible consensus as they are able. This is all part of caring for one another while witnessing in and to the world.

10. *Justice-active congregations, knowing that they are "elected" to be different, view the church's reality in a dialectical-critical way.* A dialectical-critical view of the church faces up to the congregation's ambivalence. Every particular church as a fallible community of sinners shares many of the standard characteristics of social groups. A dialectical-critical view of the church in society makes use of behavioral science research to expose the problematic of congregations and larger church bodies, while evaluating these findings with theological eyes. A functional, pragmatic analysis shows the con-

gregation to be a voluntary association with which people affiliate for popular and personal reasons well summarized by Barbara Brown Zikmund. Among the popular reasons for church attendance and support are that the church is a keeper of values, a helpful service organization, a place to belong, an insurance policy, and a cultural confirmer. Among the personal reasons for belonging are to seek the church's support through life's rites of passage, help in times of crisis, and satisfaction of one's special interests—whether inspirational, intellectual, aesthetic, or community-oriented.[7] These typical reasons for church membership illumine the pressure on congregations to conform to individualism, privatized faith, and moralistic piety.[8]

Those who reflect in a dialectical-critical spirit on the New Reformation church remain alert to what people naturally want while putting this functional analysis in theological-ethical context.[9] Thus leaders of justice-active congregations can move effectively into the gap between what laity often expect versus what the church is called to become, interpreting the special mission of *this* church to old and new members and the next generation. They recognize that many members have never before made a "contract" or covenanted to do anything significant in society through the church. *Points 1 through 9 indicate the combination of moves that justice-oriented and -active congregations make to change the contract by covenanting with members and friends for mission.*

Congregations move in this direction to the extent that they go beyond personal faith-inspiration to structure opportunities for significant social engagement into all aspects of their life and thought.[10] (A seminary has parallel "contract" problems. In gathering all who come to study or are appointed to teach, it must forge a community consensus or educative ethos to undergird its "mission.")

Implications of This Praxis for Theological Education

What implications can be drawn from this review of the distinctive habits or quality praxis of justice-active congregations? This chapter asks "what are you doing and where are you going?" of theological education with particular awareness of requirements for faithful, effective social ministry in 1990s North American parishes. The concern is theological education for public ministry in an ecclesial context that cares about social transformation and occupies public space.

The educational mission of the seminary community that would meet the eco-justice church highlights both the how and the what of new competencies to be learned. First, regarding the how, it is apparent that all the classic and modern departments of theological education show up interactively (seldom separately) in the real life and mission of socially engaged congregations. This is obvious enough for studying Bible, theology, ethics, history as part of what parish leaders are supposed to "know." Actually these classic fields of theological study come into play at every point in faithful parish praxis, but not often as distinct subjects of study. In ecclesial praxis they are mixed together. But that is equally the case for practical field concerns. Implication: course work that continues to stay, for the most part, in separate fields of theological study will not help much to equip leaders for eco-justice ministry in church and society.

Also, regarding *what* is taught, notice the range of knowledge and skill that any leader of a justice-active congregation needs. And notice that it is *not* at root mere "how to" stuff. A redefinition of "core" requirements is very much in order if the seminary is to journey with the eco-justice church in its local/global embodiment, while avoiding both the Scylla of subject-matter archeology and Charybdis of pastor-chaplaincy training. One important step toward defining that new core is to spend time pondering dilemmas and implications that surface in justice-active parish praxis. (This discussion is keyed to points 1 through 10 in the preceding section.)

1. What moves should be made in seminary education to remove ideologial blinders and break through social insulation as well as conventional moral reasoning? Those preparing for professional ministry who would lead others toward

repositioning must discern the social location "where they (we) are coming from." Given a privileged ethos or neighborhood residential base of most previous congregational experience, geographic relocation and cross-cultural experience can help students learn how to reposition themselves. With whom they minister and reflect also matters. An emerging problem, however, is that more of our church members are increasingly insulated and ideologically "conservative." What steps should seminaries take with pastor-supervisors and officers of congregations in which students are doing field work to deal directly with their mutual crisis of location? This question only illustrates the responsibility to foster open dialogue and to develop a required Social Ministry Education component (comparable to Clinical Pastoral Education in its expectations and supervisory qualifications).

2. How can we introduce and help students develop trenchant social analysis that has contextual ethical coherence and prophetic thrust as well as method-competence? One facet is learning to "see from the other's point of view." For both/and people the *others* to consult must include not just the powerful, but all four kinds of "experts." Beyond exposure learning we also need to teach/learn a disciplined process to assess social realities and competing ideologies encountered in the give and take of theological education and ministry. Emphasis on this practice seems all the more necessary for today's religious adherents whose habitual style is to feel it emotively more than to analyze it socially (a logical outcome of emotivism in religion, ethics, and politics).[11] Seminary curriculum should be assessed for how well it equips students to do coherent social analysis.

3. As for the task of *hermeneutics* (interpreting faith and mission in light of ecclesial origins, current events, and our experience), how should biblical literature and church traditions be approached? What key theological themes and historical developments deserve prominent attention in core seminary study? How do current events and our social experience shape theological thinking and speaking today?[12] And

how can New Reformation discourse move beyond the faith community into public life?

4. Seminaries, of course, engage "current issues." But social ministry is not the sum of issue concerns. Where does disciplined focus on strategy and styles of public ministry come into play so that something more than current issue orientation (or avoidance) occurs among students? How can current mission and common ministry (note 10 outlines the latter) become a dynamic subject of seminary education early enough to shape basic Bible, theology, ethics, and history courses? We can no longer build curriculum on the outmoded assumption that first you get the theology straight and then you get some practice. But since there is much more praxis rhetoric than there are good practical models available for seminary reflection, what actual praxis will students experience? In what settings?

5. The New Reformation makes the nature of authentic ecclesial life a topic of intense theological interest to be illumined by biblical-historical study as well as systematic reflection and practical experience. A lively ethic of being church comes into view when we ask, "What is the church to be and do in this time and place?" (There's a focus for core study!) The discussion of justice-active parish practice in point 5 above identifies some current ethical dimensions of the congregation's being and doing. Is it too much to suggest that the church's institutional life (those communal gerunds that express key values) and transforming social action (on the service-reform-resistance continuum) receive explicit attention in seminary courses? (As a bonus, such study would provide fresh opportunity for ideological critique.)

6. Each of the modes of parish life that make up a whole approach to public ministry is a subject worthy of seminary course work, at both M.Div. and D.Min. levels, to explore historical theological "roots" and develop practical skills. Modes that focus on lay ministry, public policy advocacy, community organization, and corporate responsibility have

recently received scant seminary attention, and almost nowhere in theological education can ministry modes be explored as a dynamic set. An ideal mix of course participants will include some "lay" leaders of congregations, learning along with prospective or ordained clergy.

7. Recognition that a justice-active congregation typically majors in one priority social mission concern and one significant community-building initiative should prompt the seminary community to examine the approach to social involvement it models. Does the prevailing pattern of seminary course work and community life help students learn how to "major" in quality social mission that has global and local dimension? If so, how is it structured?

A related difficulty that emerges from reviewing twenty years of social involvement by theological education is a tendency of seminaries to concentrate on either the local or the global, but not on both. Two decades ago urban training and community organization were conscious concerns of theological education; now they are displaced by creative efforts to develop global awareness through cross-cultural learning.[13] Global consciousness was a needed advance, but it has not translated into effective local and regional leadership training to grapple with this urgent social task of the 1990s church.[14]

8. Many seminaries are well positioned to foster ecumenical experience, which we know firsthand is a positive contributor to social ministry commitment and leadership. This process counteracts a regressive trend toward denominational parochialism. Not only have progressive denominations been turning inward as they worry about institutional survival. Pastors—and even seminaries—have accepted a privatized and psychologized model of parish ministry that focuses too much on meeting the needs of members of the flock. But there are "other sheep not of this fold." Positive seminary movement toward ecumenical study has yet to grapple with the special responsibilities of *geographic* ecumenicity—parish connectionalism at the community level

that works interdenominationally and coalitionally. Denominations now are remarkably indifferent to secular or interfaith alliances and are less supportive of ecumenical agencies. Yet, given the weakened state of our communions, little important work for eco-justice will occur without more parish leaders and regional church officers who value and are skilled in ecumenical and coalitional work.

9. I noted several important trends in a reconception of member, officer, and clergy roles. In a patriarchal culture and paternalistic church these must be fought for. Each new cohort of students and teachers has to learn all over again a practical theory and style of mutuality, shared expertise, partnership in ministry, as well as the "scientific" dynamics of leading voluntary organizations. Feminist impulses of the New Reformation have helped to make theological educators and students more alert to the justice character of our symbols, language, and leadership styles. But there is considerable backsliding on this front, just as there has been in the struggle for racial justice.

10. One intended outcome of seminary education is to mature in dialectical-critical understanding of the church. But prophetic nerve tends to be cut, and ecclesial "election" obscured, as seminarians learn how to fit into the parish as it is. The consequence of electing grace is that we are empowered to share Christ's suffering love for the world and to walk with the marginated in costly action for the common good. How can theological education overcome the syndrome of parish field work that distances seminarians from issues and ethics of Justice, Peace, and Integrity of Creation, reinforcing their avoidance of, rather than empowering them to undertake, public ministry?

What shall seminaries do to help students comprehend a New Reformation ecclesial paradigm of public ministry?

8

Developing Eyes and Ears for Social Ministry

Terence R. Anderson

I want to begin this chapter by stating several assumptions. First, I assume that "social ministry" belongs to the entire church, the whole people of God. That ministry is faithfully to serve and bear witness in every area of life to God's mission. God's mission in the world is nothing less than the redemption of all creation, the realization of shalom out of brokenness and chaos—a wholeness and harmony that flows from God and reflects God's character. Shalom entails the right relationship of all with God and embraces justice, well-being, health, security, concord between peoples and groups, harmony with and within nature, inner peace. In short, shalom is a condition that evokes from creation delight in and praise of God. As Psalm 85 (10–13) so marvellously puts it:

> Steadfast love and faithfulness will meet; righteousness and peace will kiss each other. Faithfulness will spring up from the ground, and righteousness will look down from the sky.

Yea, the Lord will give what is good, and our land will yield its increase. Righteousness will go before God, and make God's footsteps a way.

Shalom as "God's resolve for all of creation" comes through Jesus Christ as God's gift, and the appropriate response is faith as trust. Yet it also comes as God's call to serve God in this mission. The appropriate response is faithful obedience. I like the way the Presbyterian Church puts it: "No sphere of creation or culture is exempt from God's dominion, and in them all God is to be glorified by the obedience of faith and of faithful service.[1]

Second, I assume that the ultimate goal of all theological education is to foster an encounter with the reality of this God who is revealed in Jesus Christ and whose spirit is currently working for shalom in this world. But in addition, theological education in the seminaries and theological schools has the more specific objective of equipping people designated by the church to enable it to fulfill God's call to serve in the mission of shalom.

Third, by qualifying the term ministry with the phrase "socially responsible," I assume that we are indicating a concern that certain aspects deemed integral to it are missing or in jeopardy in the current practice of the churches. It cannot mean that the church is socially uninvolved. The church's beliefs and religious practices continue to impact wider society and have structural implications for social life as well as personal well-being. Societal consequences may not always be readily apparent and certainly are frequently not what was intended by the churches, but they are nonetheless very real. Surely this is one clear lesson we have learned from Karl Marx, Max Weber, Sigmund Freud, and company.[2] I assume, therefore, that the issue is not the extent of the church's social involvement, but rather whether it discerns clearly the nature of that involvement, the societal consequences of its beliefs and practices, and takes responsibility for these in the sense of seeking to make its impact and witness faithful to God.

But in what ways is the church of our time and context remiss in this regard? Does it tend to see God's promise of shalom only in certain of its aspects or dimensions, neglecting especially the promise of and call to justice, human concord, and harmony with nature? Or is it that the church, while attending to the many aspects of shalom, compartmentalizes them so that often its witness to one, say justice, is done in a fashion that violates its witness, say, to harmony with nature? Or is the difficulty rather that the church, in bearing witness to God's promise of shalom, wishes to restrict that promise to certain groups? Or do we see the current problem not so much as the church reducing the full orb of God's mission, but as the church failing to witness to it in all areas of life, neglecting especially the public aspects?

Whatever one's answer, one is led to ask further: Is theological education preparing people for ministry in a fashion that aids and abets such inadequacies either intentionally or unintentionally, or in a manner that equips people effectively to assist the church in recovering its full ministry?

Mind-Set, Character, and Selective Learning

The entities of theological education that determine whether or not we will adequately prepare people for socially responsible ministry include the curriculum, the faculty with their particular loyalties as well as their theories and approaches to their respective disciplines, the teaching methods used, and the social and spiritual ethos of the school. But I would like to focus in this chapter on another factor: the mind-set and character that students bring to preparation for ministry and how that affects what is learned and retained. Depending on the particular commitments, interests, dispositions of any group of students, some aspects of the curriculum, certain knowledge and skills needed for ministry will be welcomed and readily acquired, whereas others will be resisted, downplayed, ignored, or found difficult to acquire. When these rejected or resisted learnings (competencies, personal qualities, and commitments) are required by the curriculum, they are viewed by some students as major stumbling blocks or barriers.

A colleague at a school in Canada spoke a few years ago

about a group of religiously conservative students who, having taken all the required biblical courses in the curriculum, wrote at the end of their final papers that although they had learned the historical/critical method only because it was required for graduation, they viewed it as disrespectful of scripture and subversive of the faith, and would abandon it at graduation. Also, I remember when a considerable number of students were coming to seminary so involved in social action and so convinced that what they were doing was right that critical reflection in ethics was viewed by them as unnecessary. They wanted ethics only for moral legitimation. The study of history was endured only for the sake of passing exams.

Students' agenda, questions, and expectations lead, then, to selective appropriation of curriculum, and affect what is retained. They also shape what we teach and the way we teach. The impact made on one's teaching by the presence of black students, women students, overseas students comes to mind.

Social Context, Analysis, and Learning Filters

One of the major difficulties in preparing people for socially responsible ministry is that the current religious and social milieu of North American societies fosters perceptions, dispositions, beliefs, and knowledge that, in certain key respects, are contrary to those essential for socially responsible ministry. Many students come to seminary, thus, with real, although usually unconscious, blocks to learning, even assuming that both the curriculum and the faculty deem such matters as important.

This is not the place to analyze that milieu. There is a rich literature that helps us to understand some of the dynamics of modern North American societies that work against church involvement in the full social dimensions of its ministry. Let me note here three *major* motifs: (1) the separation of nature from supernature, confining religion and the spiritual to supernature and assessing nature as a closed entity of material forces (part of our heritage from the Enlightenment); (2) the "possessive individualism" characteristic of capitalism; and (3) the bureaucratization and the peculiar cognitive style characteristic of modernity that accompanies advanced industrialization.[3]

A meeting of the leaders of the Nisga'a National and Pierre Elliot Trudeau when he was still prime minister of Canada provided a marvellous vignette of all three of these characteristics. The topic was the Nisga'a peoples' ancestral lands. Trudeau viewed the task as drawing up a legal *contract* regarding property title and brought with him a bevy of bureaucrats and a bank of lawyers. He was surprised that the Nisga'a elders brought only their priest. He asked, "Why on earth did you bring your priest to such an occasion as this?" (no doubt suspecting paternalistic control by the Anglican Church). The Nisga'a, in turn surprised by Trudeau's astonishment, replied, "Because the matter of land is a sacred and religious matter," and they had assumed that what was to be discussed was a possible *covenant* in regard to it.

There are, however, distinctive variations of these social currents as well as additional ones peculiar to more immediate contexts. Good social analysis can aid our understanding of these and of course is widely acknowledged as an essential aspect of social ethics and as crucial for socially responsible ministry. But the point to be understood here is that such social analysis can help students to discover and understand the perceptual lenses and "habits of the heart" that they are likely to bring to seminary programs and that shape their learning.

I am convinced that providing students with the tools and skills for critical social and self analysis is essential for responsibly addressing this crucial problem of selective perception and learning as well as fundamental to the actual practice of a socially responsible ministry. These tools should be offered to students early enough in their programs so that they can be used by them to discover for themselves some of the social and personal factors that affect their approach to learning and formation for ministry.

This kind of self-understanding that includes awareness of

one's own social location and insight into that context is not easily acquired. It is more familiar to minority groups who are pressed toward it by their social circumstances. But middle-class people are more accustomed to self-knowledge primarily based in only individual psychological terms. In light of this, the temptation is to impose a social analysis on them and explain to them why they have certain filters in their perception. But such dominating styles of social analysis are both distorting and morally inappropriate.

Social analysis and critical thought entail a disciplined method and the careful use of social sciences, but throughout the underlying theories, applications, and conclusions are hermeneutical judgments that involve beliefs and values in a way more akin to art than the precise measurements possible in quantitative science. Pretentious claims of empirically verifiable "scientific truth" for any single approach of social analysis, therefore, is unwarranted and masks particular beliefs and loyalties. Such claims facilitate the use of social analysis as a weapon of attack and control by those purporting to be the scientific elite who alone have the correct analysis. Not only is this oppressive, but it in turn generates resistance to the whole enterprise and perhaps reciprocal attack with the same weapon. Again, minority groups are familiar with such uses of social analysis to identify them, categorize them, and exclude them. But it has been used in the same way by some radicals against all people of middle-class origins or even to dismiss those with a more conservative religious background.[4]

What is needed in theological education, therefore, is cultivation of an art of social and self analysis that helps us not only to discover who "our people" are and their social location, but also critically to own our people. Such "critical ownership" avoids angry rejection of self and people along with romantic flight to another people, on the one hand, and passive acceptance of the current practices and social location of one's people on the other. It helps us to see the possibilities of "positioning ourselves" differently.[5]

Such an art of social and self analysis requires not only an awareness of its hermeneutical nature and the best scientific and theological analytical tools available, but also a "context of grace" that reflects the judgment, forgiveness, and new possibilities of God's grace to all.[6] I hope that students would feel not attacked, but challenged, not rejected, but supported in bearing the conflict and pain that goes with all self-discovery. I hope that the ethos would engender hearing a word of judgment, repentance, and renewal to their own particular people, race, gender, class, and era. An ecumenical environment that includes men and women of different cultures, classes, and ages enhances these possibilities.

I have been arguing that critical appropriation of one's own people and self is essential if students are to discern and appropriately assess their approach to the curriculum and the kind of learning selectivity that they will exercise in *preparation* for socially responsible ministry. But it is also vital for *practicing* such a ministry. I recall my first meeting with a Cherokee elder who later was to become a close friend. He led me in a lengthy discussion about my ancestry and the role of my people in society. Much later, when we were good friends, he explained to me that through that conversation he had sought not only to know me, but also to test my reliability as an ostensible supporter of Native land rights. He was checking to see if I both knew about and critically owned my people. If I did not, he would assess me as an unreliable ally.

Further, the approach to social analysis in which people are encouraged to develop it themselves as an art in a context of grace, as opposed to an approach that foists on people a particular analysis, provides a good model for ministry in the church. Can we enable students to enable in turn congregations, and possibly people's movements, to discover their own social location and the factors that hinder them from faithfully serving God's mission? Or will we instead generate a claim of exclusive expertise in social analysis that leads to the arrogant use of this as a weapon to put recalcitrant congregations in their place, or to tell people's movements who they are and what they must do?

In summary, good social and self analysis under the challenge of the gospel should reveal the mind-set, perceptions, and commitments that students generally in our society are likely to bring to a seminary curriculum and why. When such analysis is done by students themselves, it should help them to discern more precisely what qualities of character and competencies needed for socially responsible ministry they are likely to have difficulty in acquiring and why.

Learnings Caught in the Current Filters

In what follows I shall address the same matter of selective learning from yet another approach. From the viewpoint of an educator, what qualities of character and competencies needed for socially responsible ministry do many students currently in seminary tend to filter out, what learnings do they resist or seem to have barriers against acquiring? I have selected five. This selection does not come from research documented with surveys based on careful sampling, in-depth interviews, and the like. It comes only from observations out of my own experience and context, but I hope that the list might open up a line of inquiry for further discussion. I shall also point to some possibilities for overcoming the barriers.

Political and Economic Institutions as an Aspect of the Church's Ministry

One learning central for a socially responsible ministry with which many students currently seem to have difficulty is understanding that political and economic institutions are an aspect of the church's ministry. There are strong currents in the religious climate of our time that regard with despair or indifference this world or "passing age" to use the New Testament phrase, or to use more pedantic terms, "the total powers of human activity and results superimposed on the natural environment." Social institutions and culture are seen only as the backdrop for God's redemption of human souls. Society's significance in this view lies only in the fact

133

that it provides the setting for people to relate personally to God in Christ and thus receive salvation in the "age to come." Despite this climate I do not find many students seriously tempted by other-worldliness. The this-worldly aspect of socially responsible faith and ministry is not a stumbling block. On the contrary there seems to be a readiness to embrace the conviction that society, with its institutions, cultures, and values, is itself, along with individuals, included in God's redemptive purpose and activity.

Nor does the difficulty with political and economic institutions necessarily reflect an intransigent individualism, for there is great interest in acquiring knowledge and skills for dealing with the cultural aspects of our society, its values, mores and customs, myths and beliefs. The tendency of a previous era to focus almost exclusively on the therapeutic and social service aspects of ministry to the neglect of concerns for justice and social action is not operative here. There is, on the whole, a high interest in enabling the *diaconia* aspect of the church's ministry and mission to address public matters with a concern for justice; thus the familiar propensity to separate public areas of life off from the responsibility of the church is not the problem.

Rather, the selectivity in learning seems to come at the point of which features of public responsibility are given attention. The tendency is to restrict the public responsibility of the church to shaping the character and ethos of society, especially in regard to matters of sexuality, marriage, family, alcohol and drug abuse, crime, business and professional ethics. Political and economic concerns may be dutifully acknowledged as important, and specific issues like unemployment generate much concern. However, most students currently screen out of their basic, operative understanding of regular parish ministry the notion that it includes enabling the church to tackle such problems by participation in public policy formation. Even more foreign is the belief that the church has a responsibility to tend regularly to political and economic institutions, rather than addressing them only as negative factors when engaged in a particular issue. Consequently acquiring knowledge and skills relevant for such a task is given low priority and is often resented when the curriculum requires it.

Perhaps the problem is partly that academic and political institutions appear so large and distant, immune to the influence of ordinary people. This is not helped by the fact that social sciences most familiar to students entering ministry are often psychology and sociology, rather than economics and political science. Their philosophical background is more usually in the areas of epistemology and language analysis, rather than in political philosophy. Further, few models of the church in a post-Christendom era tend to economic and political institutions apart from particular crises. Incidentally the most promising sign in British Columbia in this regard is the growth of community economic development in the face of the current recession. Destitute communities that organize themselves into producer cooperatives and find funding through forms of alternative investment offer promising scope for the church to participate in fostering new experiments and alternative ways of organizing our economic life.

Theological schools need, therefore, to be especially imaginative if they are to overcome the current barriers—whatever their source—to students viewing the tending of political and economic institutions as part of the church's ministry, and so fully engaging the relevant competencies.

Disposition of Solidarity

A quality of character essential for socially responsible ministry that students currently have great difficulty in acquiring is the disposition of *hesed*, or solidarity, a distinctive kind of caring.[7] There is ready acceptance of the widely held belief concerning God's "strategic concentration on the poor."[8] There is genuine concern for the poor and dispossessed, those who are made invisible or marginalized. Students, on the whole, do not seem to block on moving from a service orientation to a social justice orientation in acting out their concern. But the disposition of solidarity does seem to present problems both in terms of students understanding what *hesed* or steadfast love entails and in their developing abiding relationships of solidarity with the poor and dispossessed.

One barrier to such learning is the propensity of many, especially middle-class students, to substitute loyalty to an abstract ideal or cause or ideology for an enduring relationship of loyalty (*hesed*) to people. Sometimes this is embellished by a romantic attachment to the anticipated high drama of the clash between forces of "light and darkness"! A feminist theologian was recently relating with some sadness how, when she had finished describing to her class the way in which her own congregation had managed to adopt inclusive language in liturgy in such a fashion that all experienced it as liberating, one woman student expressed disappointment that there had been no fight!

A group of theological educators visited an inner-city parish that is engaged in creative work with low-income and impoverished peoples. Several theological students were working there in a field education placement. The description of the parish work and participation and struggle for justice presented by the veteran worker of the parish disturbed, challenged, enlightened, and moved us. However, the presentation by the students, so similar in content and message in many ways, depressed some of us. Why? These students had certainly discovered the social dimension of ministry. Their strong passion for justice was heartwarming. But the impression that several of us had in that brief encounter was that students had been converted to a cause, and exhibited all the zeal and loyalty to it that are often displayed by religious converts. Their newfound social cause seemed to be almost a religious substitute looked to for meaning, purpose, and direction, whereas the loyalty, the "steadfast love" of the veteran staff person was obviously to the impoverished parishioners and his relationship with them in their struggle for justice. Any "cause" was subservient to that solidarity.

Working with the Haida, Nisga'a, and Dene on aboriginal land rights has helped me to discover how, from the angle of vision afforded these peoples struggling for justice, it is easy to perceive the difference between allies whose loyalty or *hesed* is to the people and their empowerment, and those whose loyalty is to an ideology or cause. The latter kind of allies seem insensitive to the diversity of stories and needs of different peoples in their struggles, and therefore attempt to homogenize them so they fit what supports ideological assumptions about *the* liberating scenario (i.e., the categories of their own cause—maximizing individual choices or victory of the proletariat and the like). Their support is provisional and depends on whether or not a particular Nation of Native People fits the frame and serves the ends of the cause.

On the contrary, those allies who offer genuine solidarity believe that their own well-being and destiny is intimately bound together with the Native people who are involved in the struggle. Such allies may be able to offer a particular assistance at a particular time because of their current position (as the word *hesed* implies), but they in turn have needs that Native people may, in another setting, be able to meet. The loyalty to one another is enduring, and support is reliably forthcoming not only during times when (as one elder put it) there may be an "Indian fad."

My depression regarding those students doing field work in the inner-city parish, I realized on reflection, was that they exhibited none of these qualities of solidarity. I fear, therefore, that they are unlikely to have in the future an enduring, socially responsible ministry. I could not envisage them enabling a congregation to discover its own socially responsible ministry, but suspect that they would simply seek to convert the congregation to their cause with the predictable result of frustration and probable abandonment either of the parish or of the social dimension of their ministry.

Another aspect of solidarity with which students currently have difficulty is the spiritual grounding of this way of caring. The tendency—once again especially in middle-class students—is to ground commitment to and support of the dispossessed in guilt or in personal alienation rather than in response to God's steadfast love for us, which in biblical understanding is the only true and enduring ground for solidarity. How do we foster the kind of spirituality that enables students to transmute guilt into repentance and

137

joyful faithfulness? How in our agenda of fostering personal growth in students do we enable them to begin to sort out alienations bound up with sin and those appropriate to a righteous anger?

The quality of "being alongside" a people in their struggles is yet another attribute of solidarity that currently poses difficulties for students. People who are attracted to ordered ministry and who are seeking to emulate Jesus Christ seem particularly tempted to a kind of messianic complex or rescuer form of caring. Instead of *serving* the Emancipator, they try *to be* the Emancipator. The posture of the "Great Emancipator," however tempered by an enlightened understanding of justice, strongly conflicts with the posture of solidarity that respects the people and their ability to define their own needs and set their own agenda for social change.

Nearly as inimical to solidarity is the posture of subservience sometimes cultivated by those seeking to free themselves from the emancipator syndrome. The temptation is mistakenly to identify loyalty with uncritical adulation, which, combined with not "owning one's people," can lead to messianic expectations of a given class, nation, or people. Subservience is frequently hammered into those accustomed to being subjected to the emancipator syndrome. For this group, developing solidarity becomes troublesome in a different way. Is it really possible, they ask, to trust the proffered support and loyalty of those outside one's group? That one's own marginalized people have something to offer in a relationship of mutality is also hard to believe.

Basic Posture Toward the Prevailing Social System   *endorsement v. repentance*

Understanding and choosing a morally appropriate basic posture toward the political/economic system and cultural ethos are other kinds of learning integral to preparation for socially responsible ministry that tend to be screened out by the prevailing filters of most students. Because North American societies are dynamic, the question proving so difficult for many to face is more accurately stated as "What should be our posture toward the current direction of social change?" A rough typology of possible responses may hone the issue. I suggest two main options, each with variations. The first might be labeled *endorsement,* and assumes that the current direction of social change should be positively embraced. One variation of this is *uncritical support.* This posture is frequently operative in those who have thought little about the matter.

Another variation of this endorsement posture toward the current direction of social change is *critical support.* This view is that although we are not in the ideal Christian society, we are moving in the right direction. What we need is more of the same. Not everything that happens along our current path of change is desirable. Important modifications in political, economic, and cultural conditions need to be made, but on the whole the general course on which our society has been and continues to move is the right one.

The second major option is that the basic posture toward the current direction of social change should be negative, a firm no. This might be called the *repentance posture,* and the claim of those Christians who opt for it is that the direction of economic change and the cultural ethos must be altered. The choice between this posture and the endorsement one is a major watershed dividing Christians. Indeed overestimating the significance of this choice for ministry would be difficult. Two illustrations will suffice. The approach to social justice is radically different depending on one's posture to the current order. Justice for northern Native people or the Quebecois, for example, when viewed from the endorsement position, is understood in terms of enabling these groups to "get on board" and with a fair share be assimilated into current directions of development. Justice for these same groups when viewed from the repentance posture is understood more in terms of development in light of their challenges, and together searching for a different path that takes seriously our diverse cultures.

Pastoral care, to provide another illustration, when approached from an endorsement position is primarily comprehended in terms of enabling hurting wounded people to cope more effectively perhaps by self-assertion with the changing demands and values of our culture. From the repentance posture, however, pastoral care is approached as enabling wounded people to take responsibility in terms of their own faith commitments for altering the direction of change of society's demands and values.

variations on repentance

There are, of course, several variations of the posture of repentance, each with quite different expectations for ministry and mission, and the preparation for them. The first variation is an outright *rejection* of the current direction of social change. Christians who take this viewpoint seek to withdraw as much as they can from society and to establish alternative communities that might be a foretaste of the new society to come. One thinks of Hutterites and other Christian commutarian experiments.

2

A second variation might be described as *revolution.* This approach clearly says no to the current social system but clearly says yes to some revolutionary program that would form a new social system. Those Christians who espouse this viewpoint see us as being, in effect, exiles in a foreign Egypt ready for the exodus. Some of the Christian liberation movements in Latin America are examples of this posture toward quite a different society than our own.

3

A third variation may be described as *resistance.* The no to this society and its current direction of change persists. We are indeed captives in Egypt, but there is no hope of an exodus in terms of this viewpoint. As one writer puts it, "for us, the world middle class, who are neither poor nor belong to the power elite, . . . [the call] is to resist the path to destruction." No socialist or other form of new society is envisaged by this approach. No hope for a mass movement. The posture is one of patient stubborn resistance to the current directions of change. Examples of this can be seen in parts of the Roman Catholic left and in the Pacific Life Community.[9]

4

A fourth variation of the repentance posture may be named *radical change.* This approach is radical because it calls for going to the very root of our society and fundamentally

140

altering the basic direction in which we are moving. It is not reformist. It differs from the rejection viewpoint, however, because it sees some important desirable aspects in our society, past and present, that should be preserved. It differs from the revolution no-yes in believing that although it is clear what new direction we should seek for society, the program and means for effecting that new course are less clear. No existing ideology or social movement sufficiently incarnates the new direction to warrant a Christian endorsement. This brings it close to the resistance variation, but radical change, unlike that viewpoint, affirms at least the possibility of significantly altering our society and Christian responsibility for attempting with others to formulate and effect concrete alternatives.

There are other options, I am certain, although where I work, most students I encounter these days have an operative posture of either critical support or the resistance variation of repentance. The Nisga'a and Haida tend to have a critical support posture toward their own societies and a posture toward the dominant society of either the resistance or the radical variation of repentance.

Discerning one's operative posture to the prevailing social system and direction of change—let alone critically assessing it in light of the gospel—is at the best of times emotionally laden, challenging, and morally crucial. Just now it seems especially onerous for students. Can we find creative and responsible ways for them to address these matters? By creative and responsible ways I mean a method and style that meet the following four criteria. First, a way that does not encourage flight from this difficult question so that students are left free to continue with an unexamined posture toward the social order. Second, a method that assists students to be honest with their own operative posture rather than simply adopt the rhetoric and position of whatever is regarded in the school as the "correct posture." Third, a mode that mitigates against the tendency of some who identify one particular posture alone as being compatible with social ministry per se, regardless of context. That kind of closure merely encourages those with a different posture to abandon any

141

intentional social ministry. Fourth, a method that makes possible a hard testing of one's operative posture in light of the demands of the gospel.

So far, I have identified three learnings that tend to get screened out by the prevailing filters that people bring to seminary. If people are to break through some of these filters and adequately prepare for a ministry that will enable the church to serve the full orb of God's mission, a significant relationship with some group of dispossessed people organized to pursue justice is necessary, although not sufficient. Exposure to the unorganized poor or victims may evoke pity, compassion, righteous anger but may well not challenge and instead even enhance the rescuer style. Likewise, relating to those organized to pursue justice but who themselves are not poor may strengthen the rescuer style rather than solidarity. A relationship with organized poor, on the contrary, brings one face to face with larger economic and political institutions and provides possibilities for impacting them in a context that also facilitates critical reflection on one's operative posture toward the current system. If at least some of that group are Christian, critical reflection in light of the gospel is greatly facilitated.

I first caught a glimpse of the educational power of a relationship with the organized dispossessed in the late '60s, when a number of seminary students were actively involved with the Southern Christian Leadership Conference in Virginia. Currently the Vancouver School of Theology is moving into a partnership with several Native church organizations that are involved in preparing Native people for ministry. A significant portion of those Native people are also active in leading their people in the struggle for land rights and self-government. Although most of their training is done in their own context, we are experimenting with a program whereby they periodically come to the seminary and both teach our students and share in some intensive courses with them. These are experienced Native elders and political leaders with a deep Christian piety and rich liturgical life. Already in the limited exposure the school has had, there has been provided for our non-Native students a whole new basis for engaging in the three crucial learnings discussed earlier.

The Social as a Dimension of Ministry

Perceiving the social as a dimension rather than as only one part of ministry and mission is a fourth learning to which many students are blinded. Indeed, I have found this blindness to be one of the most widespread and persistent learning barriers. Both those strongly committed to socially responsible ministry and those most resistant tend to equate it with a certain type of social action carried on by local or national task groups in the gathered church. A congregation and a clergy person are designated "social activist" according to the size and vigor of such groups. Many times students have become excited in seminary about this kind of activity only to discover in their first conventional parish how little demand there usually is for it and how little time with "regular parish duties." "Social ministry" is shelved as a youthful ideal. There appear to be major blocks in the prevailing mind-set of our culture that prevent people from seeing that every aspect of the church's life and every function that a clergy person performs has a social dimension with implications for the societal features of mission. Dieter Hessel, in his writings, has worked hard at combatting this perceptual difficulty.[10] Does the way in which we teach preaching, liturgy, pastoral care, and educational ministry contribute to the persistence of this stumbling block?[11] Perhaps one obstacle is that congregations and clergy used for training in field education usually exemplify the notion that socially responsible ministry entails only taking on *additional* roles, rather than primarily having to do with a *different way* of performing traditional functions. This problem is closely related to a fifth learning that also at the moment is obstructed.

Mission of the Laity in Dispersion

Taking seriously the mission of the laity in dispersion is the fifth learning. The word dispersion is preferable to "scattered" in describing this mode of the church's ministry because it better expresses the proper notion of both intentionality and accountability to the community, instead of individualistic witness unrelated to the community of faith. Of course, an emphasis on the ministry of the whole people of God has been current in Protestant circles since World War II and in Roman Catholicism since Vatican II. Students generally greet it with enthusiasm, and acknowledging this ministry is *de rigueur*. But in practice the ministry of the laity connotes for most, including those responsible for theological education, primarily ministry in the gathered community of faith. Of course, those preparing for a practicing ordered ministry have a certain vested interest in that emphasis, since in that setting they remain of central importance with much power and influence. The laity dispersed are laity away from clergy control! But also many laity find the notion of dispersed mission threatening because to live faithfully in a pluralistic society that is increasingly alien to Christian values is a very demanding enterprise.

Recently a person long engaged professionally in both teaching and writing in Christian ethics and sociology went into a new occupation. When asked to reflect how he now viewed his former profession, he remarked that what stood out most for him was the unreality of so much that was taught in the seminary, including by himself. It seemed remote from the actual world and options that face most laity most of the time. A good portion of my own work is teaching Christian Ethics to lay groups engaged in various professions and fields of work or engaged in some form of political action—Christian laity in dispersion. Here is where much of the church's witness to God's shalom, i.e., socially responsible ministry, is carried on well or poorly. But such laity rarely recognize that in these matters they are called to exercise their ministry in response to God's mission. Even less frequently have they experienced any recognition of this or preparation for it in their congregation. They most always lament that there is no place in the regular life of their congregation and the gathered Christian community, where this kind of reflection on the moral appropriateness of their actions can take place.

Recognizing this ministry in dispersion and then making a connection between that reality and the regular gathered life

144

of the congregation and in turn the traditional role of the clergy person seems to be difficult for most students. Failure to do so is one of the most significant barriers to formation for socially responsible ministry.

How in theological education are the barriers to these last two learnings to be addressed? Some significant relationship with laity who are intentional about the social dimension of mission in the place where they live and work is necessary though not sufficient to prepare persons adequately for a ministry that will help the church to witness to God's mission. In recent years, a short course I have given in conjunction with the intensive field education semester of our program has pointed to some interesting possibilities. As part of their field education program, students are expected to locate in their placement a lay person or group of lay persons who not only have a clear sense of mission in the place where they live and work but are specifically attempting to attend to a social structure or institution. Invariably, the first learning of students is that there are not many such people to be found and that they are difficult to discover!

However, once having found such a person the student is to "walk with that person" and learn as much about his or her work as possible, including the obstacles faced, the strategies used, the moral dilemmas encountered, the self needs that are generated when trying to carry out mission. A nurse attempting to change the structure of her ward so that it would be both more just and effective, a woman attempting to strengthen and make more equitable the institution of marriage both by working at her own marriage and in her counsel and help to other young women, an unemployed young person helping to organize a community whose main industry shut down to form a producers co-op, an elderly woman working with the community group seeking to change public policy so that the testing of cruise missiles would be banned, an engineer working at a lower level of management for a big utility who was trying to change company policy regarding the building of a dam are the kind of laity with whom students connect.

One of the unexpected yet most exciting benefits that has

145

emerged from this process is the sense of renewal and empowerment that comes to the laity involved through the simple act of recognition that they do have a ministry and mission in the place where they live and work, and some measure, however limited, of support for that. The student glimpses the possibilities of serving these servants in dispersion.

Meanwhile back in the classroom we gather and collate the list of needs identified by these laity in the very diverse situations. One cluster that clearly emerges is the need for recognition and reaffirmation that they have a call to serve in the place where they live and work. That sense of call is difficult to maintain in an often alien setting, especially if there is no recognition by the gathered community of what these laity are about or are facing. The second cluster has to do with: (a) the frequently identified need to think through the questions and challenges to their faith that arise from the difficulties and dilemmas they face "in the world"; (b) a need to think through "the place" of their particular struggle in relation to the ministry of God's redemptive activity and the struggles of others to bear witness to that; and (c) a community of believers where they can systematically reflect on the moral dilemmas that confront them in regard to the rightness of the goals they pursue and the strategies selected for achieving them. Yet another need is for support from those who are willing to bear burdens with them. Forgiveness for failure and mistakes, nurture and the binding of wounds encountered, renewal of hope are all commonly mentioned. Finally there is a cluster that has to do with acquiring skills of change agentry, of knowing how and when to testify to their faith, better knowledge of the way our society functions and the like.

None of these is surprising, but the shocking thing for most of our students is to discover that most of these laity make little connection between what goes on in the regular life of their congregation and their sense of mission and the needs that arise therefrom in the place where they live and work. The students then begin to see with new eyes what goes on in the gathered life of the parish in which they are placed. They begin to discover how the familiar roles of a clergy person in which they expect to engage—preaching, educational ministry, liturgy, pastoral care—can be shaped in a way that directly serves the kinds of needs the laity in dispersion have identified. This process has proved more effective than any other in my experience in helping students discover both the ministry and mission of laity in dispersion with all its rich possibilities, and that the "social" is a dimension of one's entire ministry and not simply one function of it.

In preparing people for a socially responsible ministry we need to consider, then, not only what should be taught, by whom and how, but the obstacles ingrained in character and mind-set to certain learnings needed for such a ministry. These are generated by the objective social conditions in which seminary students find themselves. Good social analysis and self-analysis by students will aid them in identifying such blocks so they can be scrutinized in the light of the gospel. I have identified five learnings that currently seem to be so obstructed. Others could certainly be added to the list, especially some that involve a responsible ministry to nature. But in other places and times the list may be quite different. Those engaged in preparing people to serve God's mission of shalom need to join in a common venture of finding creative ways to overcome the barriers to acquiring what is needed for that service.

9

Tradition and Change

Curricular Trends in the Recent History of Theological Education

James D. Beumler

A little less than twenty years ago theological education entered a period of questioning and change. The causes of the questioning were manifold and came from both within and without the theological academies themselves. Thinking back to the mid-1960s brings to memory some of the cultural sources of innovation: the free speech movement at Berkeley and wider expressions of the cultural iconoclasm of the college generation; the overturning of southern near-feudalism in the civil rights movement; books with such titles as *Why Johnny Can't Read* and *Death at an Early Age,* which assailed traditional education; and the fact of the war in Vietnam, whose awful truth seemed to demand a reconsideration of everything that had previously been accepted. Meanwhile in the seminaries and divinity schools a theological free-for-all was taking place as old liberals, apostles of St. Paul Tillich,

Kierkegaardians, Barthians, death-of-God and honest-to-God theologians all coexisted within the academy and anathematized one another with little discernible effect.

For nearly three hundred years there had been universal agreement that the body of divinity a minister must learn consisted of three principal fields—Bible, church history, and theology—and later a fourth, practical field. With the '60s the demands of a fractured society and the loss of what had passed for epistemological certainty about the givenness of the form of theological education came together to force a reconsideration of that form in light of the clear need to be socially relevant and responsible. The task of this chapter is to examine what came out of this process of reconsideration as evidenced in the M.Div. programs of ten selected Protestant theological institutions over the past seventeen years.*

The material that forms the basis for this kind of exploration is the public documents of the seminaries themselves: catalogs, mission statements, curricular review, and self-study documents. Their use is no substitute for having continuously been a neutral observer at each of the seminaries for the same period. But even acknowledging the limits of the historical materials, a worthwhile analysis can take place. Insofar as the institutions have tried faithfully to represent their values, hopes, goals, and conceptions of ministry in the documents that they offer to the public and to prospective students, they have left behind a record of who they claimed or hoped themselves to be. The continuities and changes in that record are one window into the nature of contemporary theological education and the focus of this paper.[1]

---

*The institutions are as follows: Pittsburgh Theological Seminary; Interdenominational Theological Center, Atlanta, Georgia; Pacific School of Religion, Berkeley, California; Wesley Theological Seminary, Washington, D.C.; Union Theological Seminary, New York City; Vancouver School of Theology, British Columbia; and United Theological Seminary of the Twin Cities, New Brighton, Minnesota; chosen because they were represented by participants at the Consultation for which my original paper was written; and three other schools—Eastern Baptist Theological Seminary, Philadelphia; Virginia Theological Seminary, Alexandria; and Luther Northwestern Seminary, St. Paul, Minnesota—subsequently chosen to represent better the range of Protestant theological education.

A Theological Curriculum for the 1970s

It is often helpful to analyze actual circumstances in terms of ideal types. In the case of theological education the analysis of recent curricula in terms of social responsibility is made easier by the existence of an actual model produced by a task force operating under the auspices of the American Association of Theological Schools. The model, entitled "A Theological Curriculum for the 1970s,"[2] although never fully implemented in any one place, did represent the best of contemporary, socially alert thinking about how theological education for professional ministry should be constructed. The model's major emphases can be summarized as follows.

Entry requirements. It was determined that theological institutions should require the following of students entering their programs:

A. A high level of understanding of human selfhood and existence; or modern social institutions and problems; or culture and religion
B. Moderate competence in one other secular category of knowledge (the three above, plus modes of understanding or science and technology) and in one of the theological categories (Bible content and interpretation, history of Christianity, and constructive theological interpretation)
C. Linguistic skill in one of the languages of academic research
D. Ability to write clearly
E. Passing a standardized test to assess the above requirements

Exit Requirements. The model envisioned the following requirements for graduation from seminary with a bachelor or master of divinity degree:

A. Demonstrated ability to reflect theologically about current social problems by producing two forty- to fifty-page papers, one in the area of major theological competency and one that deals theologically with an area of secular enterprise

B. Reading knowledge of two languages
C. Moderate knowledge of the Bible, church history, historical and contemporary Christian thought, contemporary issues confronting Christian faith, and one non-Christian religion to be assessed through a final battery of seminary tests
D. Maturity to be evaluated by the seminary in connection with work in close conjunction with a faculty member in a core group

Shared responsibility of faculty members for spiritual formation of, and encouragement of maturity in, ministry students.

Shared responsibility among departments and/or fields for socially responsible theology and ministry.

The last two emphases were the most radical departures from the status quo in theological education as it was then being done, for it cut against the increasing professionalization of subfields of theological knowledge. Biblical studies professors were in effect being asked to pay attention to the contemporary meaning and social impact of their subject matter. Church historians were being assigned the tasks of ministerial development. This came at a time when seminary teachers in their identities as scholars were under pressure from their subject matter guilds to be more like their university counterparts.

The 1968 model offered one further major recommendation: that beyond the first two levels of general theological education outlined in the emphases above, a third level of theological education take place, and that this be a level of specialization. Not unlike medical residencies, these specializations would be offered only at specifically designated "III-A Centers for Advanced Theological Education" geared to training for ministry in a particular social setting. The model envisioned one school offering advanced work in business and industry ministry, while another might be a center for "life cycle ministry."[3] The ideal curriculum thus promoted the idea that seminaries should be allowed to concentrate their energies on areas of excellence, but also called into question the ability of individual seminaries to do all things well. In this way, too, "A Theological Curriculum for the 1970s" was pushing up against cherished assumptions and institutional realities.

The ideal curriculum of the 1968 report, therefore, came as a challenge, in all senses of the word, to the theological enterprise. The analytical conclusions that follow are based on measuring the curriculum of each school against the challenging emphases set forth in the Task Force report. Even so, a close reading of the report raises some questions about the time-boundedness of the ideal curriculum. The "he" repeatedly used discussing the hypothetical seminarian in 1968 would now be "s/he" at the very least. A reexamination of the goals set in the past often reveals shortcomings but also reminds us of areas in which we have made surprising progress. We might want to factor gender issues/understanding into our contemporary analysis and ask whether seminaries are consciously equipping students to deal effectively with gender roles in the world in which they seek to minister. In any case, the use of the 1968 model is heuristic and not the final word in socially responsible theological curriculum. Indeed, comparing the actual curricula of the schools over time against the emphases of the Task Force report raises questions about that effort and the presuppositions that went into it:

- Would Spanish now be a language that we would count as being theologically/ministerially useful? Both, I think.
- In the 1968 proposal there was a great stress on evaluation. We might ask whether that was just something of the "New Academism," or one of its most constructive suggestions; whether taking a final measure of competency and maturity was a more responsible approach to determining fitness for ministry than a transcript showing a series of passed courses.

- Forty- to fifty-page papers, are they obsolete? Would we be better off preparing ministers if they were required to learn how to write a theologically adept sermon on a social problem, or an effective letter to the local newspaper on a political controversy?

As these questions may already suggest, the retrospective examination of curricular plans and realities leads to a certain cautiousness about the limitations of even the best of plans on how to train ministerial leadership for the future. At the same time it is clear that the past experiences of the ten theological schools have much to teach about what works, what does not, and what obstacles have stood in the way of effective preparation for socially responsible ministry.

Analytical Conclusions

In analyzing the ten schools' curricular emphases, several levels of appraisal can be made. These levels may be classed in terms of *Intent:* What does the institution say it's trying to do? *History:* How much change has there been curricularly anyway? In what directions has that change occurred? *Reality:* What happens apart from institutional intent and curricular encouragement or disencouragement? How do students educate themselves in fact? How does learning actually take place? How do teachers teach—in fact?

Intent. The first analytical category that must be examined in any investigation of seminary curriculums designed to determine how they are positioned with respect to a socially responsible ministry is that of intent. For if a seminary has a completely a-political, a-social conception of its own mission and purpose, it cannot be expected to convey to its students a vision of ministry as whole and irreducibly social.

One long-term, observable trend is that institutional mission statements have become increasingly complex over the past seventeen academic years. Gone are the simple, one-sentence statements that are characteristic of catalogs twenty years ago with words like ". . . is a graduate school of Christian theology which trains young men for service in the Christian church." Over the years all kinds of modifiers have crept into these descriptions: "lay and professional," "and women," "social service," "other ministries," "leadership," "enabling," "structures of society." These words and phrases indicate a change in language and a new rhetoric of academic catalogs, to be sure. But these terms are more than merely a "newspeak" for seminaries. Rather, they signal a broadened conception of the purpose of theological education. And, as the modifying words above taken from recent seminary self-descriptions suggest, that conception has grown in the direction of being more socially focused. This is true even though none of the seminaries studied has conceived of itself along the lines suggested in the second part of "A Theological Curriculum for the 1970s" and set itself out as a single "III-A Center" for advanced theological education. Instead, they have presented themselves as full-service seminaries that provide training for all these kinds of ministries. By inference, it can be concluded that all these ministries are part of "the ministry."

One of the underlying assumptions of the Task Force report was that theological education be directed at more than the mere attainment of knowledge. Knowledge was important as it figured into the larger goal of theological education: ministerial competence. The underlying premise was that theological education made competent ministers, and that the educated minister was the competent minister. Competence, of course, necessitates a mechanism for evaluation, and the degree to which the institutions have addressed this need is a concern of the next section of this chapter. But here it is appropriate to survey the categories that the seminaries have set forth as making for competent graduates because therein lie their stated philosophies of what constitutes ministry.

Two of the institutions, Interdenominational Theological Center (ITC) and Pittsburgh Theological Seminary, list nearly identical statements of abilities necessary to basic professional competence. In the words of the former institution's version, these include the following:

- The ability to understand and use with competence the basic documents of faith. . . .
- The ability to communicate orally and through written forms an adequate appropriation of scripture and religious heritage. . . .
- The ability to counsel and provide leadership in programmatic and administrative areas.
- The ability to understand in biblical and theological terms the sociological, ideological and political content of the cultures in which the church ministers.
- The ability to practice one or more forms of ministry in an appropriate progressional manner.[4]

At the Pacific School of Religion these same basic abilities are described in still more socially aware and directed terms. Based on the proficiencies for ministry offered by the faculty, the minister is one who has

Ability to draw critically on the biblical Christian heritage and the resources of contemporary society to provide for one's own spiritual formation and to give effective leadership to the Christian movement in witness and mission; Insight and skill for communicating Christian faith and ethics through [a wide range of] appropriate means; Capability, experience, and willingness to take leadership in social change on behalf of the prophetic witness of the Christian tradition and its commitment to justice and love; Knowledge, experience, and willingness to lead Christian communities in worship and to prepare laity to participate in leading worship; and, Preparation and practice in caring ministries.

Two of the other institutions have related their ministerial competence standards to curricular objectives. Thus Vancouver incorporates ministerial competency objectives into the requirements of each field of study in the curriculum. For its part, Wesley articulates objectives in the areas of "the faith of the church," "the church in the world," and "the ministries of the church" each of which are said to involve foundational

155

knowledge, competence in appropriate methods of study and interaction, and a stance or attitude that is "supportive of the overall demands of leadership and service in ordained and lay ministry." To these curricular objectives, Wesley adds

non-curricular objectives [that] reflect the Seminary's concern that those engaged in professional service to the church should be mature and growing persons: 1. Continuing growth in faith. 2. Moral integrity. 3. Psychological and emotional health. 4. Responsiveness in personal relationships. 5. Involvement in social concerns.[5]

Eastern Baptist Seminary articulates fourteen "Educational Objectives: for people having completed the M.Div. degree; the twelfth of these is the most interesting for our purposes, maintaining that a graduate from the program should be able to "Participate in contemporary life as a responsible Christian contributor and critic."[6]

A completely different approach to stating institutional intentions is offered by Virginia Theological Seminary. Its catalog contains not one statement, but several. There is a mission statement, an interpretive history of the seminary, a statement entitled "What Undergirds the Curriculum," another titled "Theological Education for Today," and an essay by a graduate, "This Business of Ministry." The total effect of these statements is to present in a narrative form what VTS seeks to be and to do, rather than in the propositional form used by most academic catalogs. From "What Undergirds the Curriculum" comes a philosophy of the two "alternative procedures" in theological education:

One is to give high priority to the content of theology as an historically-given body of tradition to be mastered. . . . The alternative procedure is to give the priority to personal appropriation not in proportion to what is given but in proportion to what the individual is capable of receiving. . . . The traditional material is of course presented in the classroom, but with more concern for the relevant than the traditional, for commitment and testimony than for orthodoxy, for personal involvement than for the acquisition of information.[7]

From this description of the alternatives Virginia goes on to describe why its choice has been primarily for the latter.

Only one of the seminaries, Union Theological Seminary, still makes no statement of what constitutes competency in ministry. On the whole, then, today's seminaries are quite explicit about the need for and commitment to inclusiveness. PSR, ITC, and Eastern even make commitments to using the life experiences brought to theological education by adult learners and to reshaping the learning process in response to changes in the composition of the student body. The seminaries are also fairly intentional in conveying the message that a complete ministry has a vital social dimension. The extent to which changes in curriculum have paralleled these good intentions are, therefore, the next issue for consideration.

History. To ask how much curricular change has moved in the direction of preparing people for socially responsible ministry is to take up the question of how much change there has been in the first place. The level of change has differed from school to school. United Theological Seminary is one case in point. In the mid-1960s United had a fairly traditional curriculum. In 1970–71, partly through the efforts of Thomas Campbell—both a United faculty member and a member of the Theological Curriculum for the 1970s task force—the seminary dropped the traditional fields for three fields of study, "Christianity and Culture," "Interpreting the Christian Heritage," and "The Church's Ministry," each with its own introductory series of courses. The new curriculum was based on Tillich's method of correlation, letting the world ask the questions. A person skilled in ministry, therefore, was one who could answer those questions theologically. United also moved to modular scheduling in which classes met for extended time periods one day a week in order to allow field trips, greater commitments to work experiences, and so forth.

During the 1970s United shifted away from the correlational model as feminist and liberation theologies created different issues to be dealt with and produced different perspectives from which to approach those issues. In 1980 the seminary established a Center for the Shaping of Values to both address lay decision makers and to coordinate within the curriculum those courses dealing with social, political, and economic topics. The Center was subsequently discontinued. Currently United once again has a curriculum review process under way. An interim report affirms that several current curricular features should be retained, including block scheduling, the integration of theory and practice, a theological emphasis on personal and social transformation, and a focus on providing competency in leadership. Apart from these affirmations, however, the curriculum is open to wide change, for United's Curriculum Review Task Force has resolved to develop its work around an ideal curriculum and not simply modify the current curriculum. To some observers, then, it would seem that United has been in a state of constant curricular change.

At the other extreme is Union Theological Seminary. Union has not had a major curriculum overhaul in the entire period examined. Its course offerings and catalog statements would be equally familiar to students of 1965 as to students of today. It has made two notable changes in its program since 1970, however. First came the abandonment of a traditional letter grade system in favor of a written evaluation and credit/no credit system applying to each course. The second change was to reinstitute a core curriculum. The curriculum contained some course options but sought to assure that all divinity graduates would have a well-formed basic knowledge and vocabulary of the traditional fields of theological learning.

Despite their different rates of change, both of these seminaries have moved in directions set out in the ideal curriculum of the 1968 Task Force. Evaluative accountability has been strengthened, and balance in knowledge has been reasserted as an educational virtue. Yet other institutions have approached the evaluation of competence in rather different ways that are also derived from goals articulated in "A Theological Curriculum for the 1970s." The Pacific School of Religion, for example, has retained letter grading and provides no other final evaluation of the work for individual courses, but has an integrative approach to determining which individual students have become proficient in the areas necessary to their vocational plans. At PSR each student must prepare a "Vocational/Academic Plan" in his or her first year. The plan serves as the working covenant between the student and PSR, and as the basis for required systematic reflection on preparation for ministry in a Middler Review and a Senior Report. This approach maximizes at least one thing that the 1968 Task Force called for, the shared responsibility of faculty members for spiritual formation of and encouragement of maturity in ministry students. Luther Northwestern also retains a letter grade system as an option, partly out of a recognition that graduate schools expect it, but allows students to choose the way they want to be evaluated by making available the further options of written evaluations and a pass/marginal-pass/fail grading system.

Vancouver School of Theology's approach toward assessing competence and the integration of social and theological sensitivities comes from another angle, although one also discernible in "A Theological Curriculum for the 1970s." At Vancouver the demonstration of competencies is divorced from course work. No grades are given for classes. Instead, each of the divisions—Biblical, Church History/Theology, and Ministry—has a list of areas of competence that must be met. In the latter two divisions the objectives often require that areas of knowledge be applied to ethical situations with pastoral sensitivity in a paper. The final year of the program also contains six integrative seminars, three of which draw on both field and academic experiences to examine the societal change dimension of ministry, church and society, and the church in mission. Finally, students must produce a paper on their own theological position for ministry in which ministry's societal aspect must be addressed. Vancouver's program, remarkably different from that of the other schools, has adopted a plan of evaluation that closely parallels the 1968 plan's exit requirement that envisioned students demonstrating ability to reflect theologically about current social problems by producing two lengthy papers addressing theological and secular problems across strict disciplinary lines. The program also evidences another emphasis of the 1968 report—that there be shared responsibility among fields for socially responsible theology and ministry. Wesley has developed another way to build shared faculty responsibility for the nature of the theological education it gives its students. Under its innovative program Wesley's faculty members actually take one another's classes.

Perhaps the level and nature of overall curricular change in these institutions in this period is indicated by the fact that it was in the year 1970 that the Eastern Baptist Seminary adopted a doctrinal affirmation entitled "Here We Stand," which, among other things, committed it to continual curricular review. The statement began, "In a time of change, confusion and erosion of old authorities, yet filled with opportunity and challenge, Eastern affirms the unchanging Christian message to the world." The affirmation went on to present reconciliation with God and others and spiritual renewal as essential prerequisites to "healing of the social illnesses that plague the world" and then presented its vision of the church, ending with a statement of the faculty's educational philosophy:

> We also want our graduates to combine certitude concerning revealed truth with searching openness to new insights, alertness to contemporary currents of thought, and flexibility in modes of action.
>
> Therefore in our teaching we purpose to conserve the truth of God without being static or uncritical to progressive teaching techniques.
>
> We propose to have a curriculum in accord with these aims and to subject it to continuing review. We seek to do all this in subjection to the gracious authority of Jesus Christ our Lord.[8]

Today this statement serves as the way in which the prospective student is introduced to the faculty, whose photographs accompany the material. Curricular change and review has been the norm and not the exception in the years since 1970, and, in the case of Eastern, a fact of which it is proud and a principle to which it is committed.

All the schools in the study have made some changes in the directions suggested by the Theological Curriculum for the 1970s Task Force report. And on the whole this change has been set within a great deal of curricular reexamination. Yet there have been nearly as many ways of doing theological education as institutions. The elements suggested by the Task Force report as critical to every theological education have been, in actual historical circumstances, broken up and used as organizing motifs for particular theological educations.

Reality. To examine the curricular emphases of the ten seminaries in the study only in terms of statements of intent and the history of curricular change would be to assume that planning for learning and learning are one and the same. The self-studies of the schools and the patterns of their programmatic changes suggest that preparation for a socially responsible ministry does not always take place along the lines envisioned by curriculum reform committees.

One can tell only a limited amount about the conception of ministry that is passed on to students through informal channels by examining the curriculum. Union Theological Seminary, with its tradition of sending high proportions of its graduates into nonconventional ministries within the culture, has accomplished this feat despite being locked into the most traditional, academic department-oriented curriculum of all. Union offers few normative judgments about what ministry should be, offers only one foundational course to explore the integration of course learning into the practice of ministry, and yet graduates a sizable number of men and women who do integrate their theological educations with social vision. This fact signals either a process of self-selection whereby theologically and politically liberal students who see ministry as a culture-transforming entity seek out an institution in which they will be ideologically at home, or the strong effect of living in the city and working in situations, be they churches, agencies, or soup kitchens, where religious ideals and ugly societal realities constantly confront one another.

In terms of providing a social dimension to students' theological insights and bridging theory and practice, field education probably plays as important a role as any activity in theological education. The fortunes of field education programs within the sample seminaries, however, have tended to be poor. In one school after another repeated crunches in finances have led to the relegation of field education to second-class status as an experienced member of the faculty is replaced by a full-time director without faculty status, who in turn is replaced by a part-time director or administrative assistant who only has time enough to match students with requests for their services. If the successful practice of social ministry is from the beginning grounded in thoughtful reflection and analysis, then enough institutional resources need to be committed to that process to provide that it will occur on a more than ad hoc basis.

One of the most striking realities to emerge in the past twenty years is that more and more theological education—particularly education for social responsibility—is taking place outside of theological seminaries. Luther Northwestern is one case in point. Its most recent catalog describes no less than twelve off-campus programs that may be taken for credit. These include a Central America/Mexico study seminar, study at seminaries in the Third World, a three-week introduction to rural ministry, an examination of church and state relations in the setting of the two Germanys, and an intensive introduction to reservation life either among the Papago or the Yaqui Indians. Students may also spend various lengths of time at the Washington, D.C., House of Studies run by the Lutheran Seminary, Gettysburg. There they are exposed to ways in which the church at various levels can approach issues of public policy. Students at all the institutions examined here have similar opportunities to learn theology in an experiential context. Students on these programs often identify these experiences as the high point of their seminary careers. Students in the House of Studies program would also come into contact with member schools of the

Washington Theological Consortium, including Wesley and Virginia Theological seminaries. This reveals another major shift in contemporary theological education; theological education is being done more ecumenically than ever before. Most theological seminaries are now in consortium-type relationships with other institutions.

Another development in contemporary ministerial education that the catalogs only hint at is the addition of Clinical Pastoral Education (CPE) to the curriculum. From the sample of seminaries in this study it would appear that requiring CPE of divinity students is more common among the more "liturgical" seminaries. But although only Luther Northwestern and Virginia require CPE of all students, all the schools make it possible for their students to take this training, and many denominations recommend or require it of candidates seeking ordination. It is doubtlessly true that the experience of CPE has better equipped parish ministers for the part of their ministries that takes place in the context of illness, hospitals, nursing homes, prisons, and crisis centers. However, a few critical questions about the consequences of this development can be voiced: Does the popularity of CPE signal that the ministry is being conceived in terms of a client- or patient-centered activity? Why is there not also something called PSE, Pastoral Social Education?

At the heart of the curriculum—offerings and requirements—there has also been a marked degree of activity. In 1969 Pittsburgh Seminary went to a completely elective system, requiring only that a minimum of fifteen hours be taken in each of the three divisions. In a self-study of the same year the seminary appraised the change:

> The adoption of the elective system has been a response to the valid desire on the part of students for more responsibility in choosing when they study what, but their choice has been limited by the implicit assumptions of the three divisions about what seminary students ought to study. This in turn reflects the assumptions which controlled the selection of faculty with their particular interests and specializations.[9]

What Pittsburgh concluded about the impact of its curriculum change might, with equal justice, be said about other seminaries' programs and curricular changes in general. Regardless of the number of times the curriculum changes, the tendency is for the same courses to reappear unchanged. On the whole, faculty members appear less resistant to program changes that require new foundational courses of divinity students—either in traditional areas or in interdisciplinary areas—than to changes that require that they change the way they teach or the courses they teach. This is humanly quite understandable. But it builds in a kind of systemic resistance to any meaningful curricular change.

A related problem quickly becomes evident to any reader of several institutions' catalogs. For the standpoint of calling for whole, socially relevant theological education, one of the 1968 Task Force's major emphases was that responsibility for socially concerned theology and ministry should be shared among departments and faculty members. When one examines the actual course offerings together with their faculty assignments, one finds that the courses that embody a social vision of ministry, or that use descriptive phrases like "and its contemporary impact," are almost invariably taught by specialists in ethics or church and society, or sometimes religious education or homiletics. Each of the schools in the study has at some point in the past seventeen years introduced one or more interdisciplinary courses to try to force an integration of traditional areas of theological study with the practice and understanding of ministry. But even these courses are overwhelmingly taught by faculty from ethics or the practical disciplines. What we see, then, is a bifurcation of theological faculties into two groups; one is committed to a wholistic view of theological education and the ministry it serves, and one prefers not to be bothered with teaching demands outside its areas of primary expertise. One can read between the lines only too well in ITC's recent Curriculum Revision Task Force Report when it detailed the terms under which faculty would be drawn in to staffing the "Foundations for Ministry" interdisciplinary introduction for students: "A major portion of the faculty is to be involved. There is to be a coordinator whose responsibility is to secure personnel and assure continued faculty participation. No faculty with full faculty status is to be exempted; participation is to be on a rotational basis."[10] A statement like that points to the problem in assuring cross-disciplinary cooperation in building toward an integrated approach toward ministerial training. ITC is not alone in the problem, perhaps just wiser in anticipating it in a new curriculum.

The decisive location of ethical thought and socially engaged theological education within so-called practical fields within the curriculum has a historical explanation. James Gustafson has pointed out that Christian ethics in the United States developed in a particularly American way and was rooted in the practical social concerns of the guilded age and the progressive era. It was in these years that theological seminaries added chairs to their faculties with names like "Applied Christianity" and "Practical Philanthropy." This legacy of the Social Gospel is still with us, for given the choice between keeping up with the issues of the day and conversing with dogmatic theology, biblical exegesis, and philosophy, most ethicists have continued to choose the former, thus setting the tone for how social concerns are located within theological education. We may point out that this is not a necessary choice, but we may not deny it is a choice that has often been treated as such.[11]

During the '70s and '80s one process has been particularly evident from the self-studies, catalogs, and internal documents of theological institutions. That process has been the rejection, readoption, and modification of required "core" curriculums. At the root of the back-and-forth debate over required cores stands the question, "What is it that every theological student should learn in his or her time with our institution?" The frequency of change in the content of that core, the vehemence of the debate while it is occurring, and the amount of time that those involved in theological education spend opposing, defending, or defining one suggest that the question is just as alive today as it was in 1968, when the Curriculum Task Force did its work. It also suggests that multiple sources are fueling the debate.

The people who seek out a theological education today are a sociologically more diverse group than their 1968 counterparts. Numbered among today's M.Div. students are many more second-career people, and many more people who have not been consistently involved with the institutional church than was once the case. PSR and ITC, as noted earlier, have recognized this and have made stated institutional commitments to using the past experience that adult learners bring to theological study. Eastern has provisions to grant a limited amount of credit for such experience. But given the fact that people will bring to seminary widely divergent experiences, the task of settling on a core of studies relevant to those people and their experiences is greatly complicated.

Concurrently, the numbers and kinds of vocational objectives of theological students have increased in the past twenty years. The problem of designing a core relevant to their future occupations was a leading factor in the widescale abandonment of required courses in the early 1970s, and has not gone away, despite the trend toward more required courses in the seminaries.

At an institutional level the matter of "what everyone should learn about the church, the world and the theological tradition" is often in tension with "what everyone should know about the subject I teach." This reflects both basic human egocentricity and a fundamental division in educational philosophy. The division between those who see education as providing knowledge and skills and those who see it as learning how to learn, or applying learned perspectives to new problems, exists in the theological academy and evidences itself in the tensions within curricular programs.

Finally, there is another reality that has impinged on the ability of even the best-designed curriculum to prepare seminarians for effective social ministry in the church and in the world. It is the classic problem of the academy as an ivory tower. There are very real limits to which anyone who is not fully in the church or in the world can prepare someone else to be in them. Yet this is what is asked of the seminary or divinity school teacher. The denominations and church members all expect that the seminaries' faculties will assess the competence for ministry of their students. Meanwhile the seminaries themselves place on their faculty members a variety of conflicting expectations; be an excellent teacher, a productive scholar, a friend and counselor to the students, and a member of five or six faculty committees and be involved with the church and community, but not to the extent that it gets in the way of your work. Clearly, when something must give, it usually does, and in the case of seminary instructors what most often "gives" is the kind of contact with the church and world that would make possible the evaluation of whether a student's education has prepared her or him for service outside the seminary.

The existence of a gulf between what a theological scholar can be expected to know in his or her capacity as specialist and what a teacher responsible for the formation of ministers must know adequately to perform that role poses a dilemma for theological education. It discloses the need for seminaries to be clearer and more realistic about expectations of their teaching staffs. It also has implications for theology as it highlights the importance of listening to the outside, to the experts, the participants, and the victims in the world, and taking the faith data they bring forth theologically as seriously as what is written in the dusty volumes that fill the libraries. In the past two decades theological education has made some strides in this direction. United's commitment to block scheduling because of the opportunities it provides for educational experiences outside the walls of the seminary is one hopeful sign in this regard. Another is Wesley's first-year program, part of which requires that students attend churches from a variety of traditions on Sunday mornings and use these experiences as the substance of discussion in their "Ecclesial Reflection Groups." The very focus of the Wesley first-year program is also a hopeful sign, for in structuring the learning around the themes of the contemporary church in global context and in local context, Wesley's program makes a decisive break with the traditional approach of foundational courses in theology that move from the Bible, through Western church history, to one's own denominational and national tradition in an ever-narrowing focus. When learning about "the church" at Wesley, the church in India is given as much attention as the Methodist Church in the District of Columbia. Despite these signs of hope, bridging the gap between the seminary and the world remains an uncompleted task.

The recent history of curricular change in theological education offers many insights for those who would reconstruct seminary training to correspond to the conviction that all ministry must be socially informed and engaged. But the greatest insight for the curriculum planner must finally be the ironic lesson that preparation for social ministry depends most essentially *not* on curriculum plans, but on people. For it is people interacting in a community of study, worship, and witness who will promote or stifle, teach and learn, and finally serve as the true context in which a social ministry takes shape.

Appendix

Seminary Self-Assessment of Education for Social Ministry

The foregoing chapters suggest priorities for curriculum focus, teaching methods, and community life to undergird theological education for socially responsible ministry. Here are twenty questions to begin *self-assessment* by a community of theological study:

1. What are the contours of dynamic, whole social ministry? What picture/model of ministry do we give students? What are its public dimensions? Is this a matter of faculty study and consensus?
2. How do community worship, ethos, and required courses help students acquire perspective on social responsibility and develop skills to make a public witness?
3. How often has this institution changed curriculum in the last 15 years? Explain major changes made in purpose. And in pedagogy.
4. What have recent graduates told us about strengths and weaknesses of their preparation for ministry? How have

seminary routines changed in response to this feedback?

5. What special social ministry needs and opportunities do the 1990s present? How prepare students for this? Besides the church, what groups in society do we serve?

6. How do we teach the social history of communities in which our students are likely to minister? What tools do we provide to analyze our contemporary setting? (Global and local reality; prevailing ideologies, etc.)

7. On what other disciplines and professional schools do we draw? With which offer cooperative programs of study? How many students take advantage of these programs?

8. From what entering knowledge to what learned content and competencies does the seminary usually take students? Which entering requirements and which exit knowledge particularly bring readiness for social ministry?

9. What is taught in each major field to undergird ministry in society? E.g., social analysis method in biblical courses, traditions of world engagement in church history, the social roots and functions of theology, and a lively ecclesiology in the practical department. Beyond content, what methods of ministry are fostered by the teaching/learning methods used by professors? Specify content and methods emphasized in required courses.

10. Identify interdisciplinary work or integrative exercises offered in each field. Near completion of M.Div. cycle, how are students encouraged toward wholistic ministry?

11. How extensively do students explore mission theology, social teachings, policies, and programs of their own communion, plus strategies/skills of social witness?

12. What kind of course work is required in ecumenics and contemporary non-Western or Two Thirds world cultures?

13. To what extent does our community encourage ethnic minority people to express their faith and life experience? Where and how does (or could) this happen?

14. Through what shared experiences or formation disciplines does our community of theological study foster/ deepen commitment to liberating social ministry and

170

highlight the main norms of lived Christian practice? How do we explore personal experiences of oppression/empowerment? How honor praxis and life experience as primary datum?

15. Beyond evaluating class work how do faculty members help students grow toward maturity as leaders in ministry? Does faculty evaluation include, and give positive significance to, social justice and peace activity? How much is mentoring valued in evaluating faculty?

16. What student groups draw participants at this seminary? How does the community do social education and action? What special events/seminars occur to deal with racism, sexism, and other problems in society and the church? What is seminary policy about using inclusive language?

17. Which of our off-campus programs develop insight into public ministry. What percentage of students participate?

18. Field world: Describe the program. Is a social dimension expected and emphasized in all or most placements? In what ecclesial settings and public sectors are students likely to acquire social ministry orientation? How build on the skills of second career students? How wrestle with the public vocation of laity?

19. How do our seminary's institutional governance and investment policies witness to justice and peace? How have decision-making powers shifted among trustees, administration, faculty, and students in last 15 years?

20. The moral life is joined and often taught covertly in the seminary community. Comment on where social ministry consciousness and ability are more likely to be blocked or developed (in the relation between courses, personnel, pedagogy, and community ethos).

In light of this self-assessment:

A. To become faithful, dynamic, and effective leaders in public life, seminary students most need to learn . . .
B. List immediate priorities for change in curriculum, pedagogy, and community life.

Notes

Chapter 1. A Social Agenda for Theological Study

1. See Arthur M. Schlesinger Jr., *The Cycles of American History* (Boston: Houghton Mifflin, 1986), chs. 1, 2, 9, 14.

2. Jose Miguez-Bonino, "Global Solidarity and the Theological Curriculum," pp. 22–24, in *Global Solidarity in Theological Education*, Report of the U.S.-Canadian Consultation at Trinity College, University of Toronto, Ontario, Canada, 1981.

3. Joseph Hough and John Cobb, *Christian Identity and Theological Education* (Atlanta: Scholars Press, 1985), p. 81.

4. James W. Fowler, "Practical Theology and Theology Education: Some Models and Questions," *Theology Today* 42 (April 1985): 1.

5. Charles M. Wood, *Vision and Discernment: An Orientation in Theological Study* (Atlanta: Scholars Press, 1985), p. 67.

6. Ibid., p. 91.

7. Arnold S. Nash, "Everything Has a Theological Angle," in *The Making of Ministers: Essays on Clergy Training Today*, ed. Keith R. Bridston and Dwight W. Culver (Minneapolis, MN: Augsburg Press, 1964), p. 272.

8. Reuel Howe, "Theological Education and the Image of the Ministry," ibid., p. 219.

Chapter 2. The Near Future of Socially Responsible Ministry

1. See especially Troeltsch's discussion, "Christianity and Religious Movements in the Graeco-Roman World," *The Social Teachings of the Christian Churches,* vol. 1 (Chicago: University of Chicago Press, Phoenix Edition, 1981), pp. 43ff.
2. See the discussion, Hans Jonas, *The Imperative of Responsibility* (Chicago: University of Chicago Press, 1984), pp. 140ff.
3. The discussion here, although not the examples, is indebted to the aforementioned book by Hans Jonas.
4. James Gustafson, *Ethics from a Theocentric Perspective,* vol. 1 (Chicago: University of Chicago Press, 1984), p. 281.
5. L. Cavalieri, "Genetic Engineering: A Blind Plunge," *The Washington Post,* May 14, 1982.
6. The distinction is E.F. Schumacher's in *Small Is Beautiful: Economics as If People Mattered* (New York: Harper & Row, 1975).
7. This immediately preceding discussion is indebted to Roger Shinn, in *Forced Options: Social Decisions for the 21st Century* (New York: The Pilgrim Press, 1985). See especially pp. 3–12.
8. A disclaimer must accompany such a bare-bones sketch as this. I do not intend to imply that Bacon, Marx, Freud, and Weber share a common mind-set! I mean only to say that there is an important point of convergence in what they, or their followers, assume, pursue, or describe: the complex we've named knowledge/power/control in the modern world.
9. David Riesman, "Some Other Observations on Community Plans and Utopia," in *Individualism Reconsidered and Other Essays* (New York: Free Press, 1954), p. 70.

Chapter 3. Black Theological Education: Dilemma and Deliverance

1. Maulana Karenga, *Introduction to Black Studies* (Los Angeles: Kawaida Publications, 1982), p. xiii.
2. Ibid.
3. Martin Kilson, "Politics and Identity Among Black Intellectuals," *Dissent,* Summer 1981, pp. 339–49.

4. Carter G. Woodson, *Mis-Education of the Negro* (Washington, DC: The Associated Publishers, 1969), pp. 5–6.

5. Langston Hughes, "The Negro Artist and the Racial Mountain," in Addison Gayle Jr., *Black Aesthetics* (New York: Doubleday, 1971), p. 167.

6. Perhaps this is why many significant studies on the black experience (e.g., the black family) are done by white scholars.

7. Harold Cruise, *The Crisis of the Negro Intellectual* (New York: Quill, 1967), p. 475.

8. Charles B. Copher, "Perspectives and Questions: The Black Religious Experience and Biblical Studies," in *Theological Education,* Spring 1970, p. 181; reprinted in Charles S. Rooks, "Vision, Reality and Challenges: Black Americans and North American Theological Education, 1959–83," in *Theological Education,* Autumn 1983, pp. 49–50.

9. ITC catalog (1986–87), p. 18.

10. Heretofore each student was required to take a course in his or her own denominational church history. Now the larger Black Church History is required for each student.

Chapter 4. The Urban Ethos of Seminary Education

1. Robert Ezra Park, "The City," in *Cities and Churches,* ed. Robert Lee (Philadelphia: Westminster Press, 1962), p. 46.

2. Max Weber, *The City* (Glencoe, IL: The Free Press, 1958).

3. Max Stackhouse, *Ethics and the Urban Ethos* (Boston: Beacon Press, 1972), p. 5.

4. Harvey Cox, *The Secular City* (New York: Macmillan, 1975).

5. Stackhouse, *Ethics and the Urban Ethos,* p. 5.

6. Max Stackhouse, *The Ethics of Necropolis* (Boston: Beacon Press, 1971).

7. See ibid., pp. 76–78.

8. Ibid., p. 92.

9. Samuel Schriner, *Thine Is the Glory* (Greenwich, CT: Fawcett Publications, 1976), p. 45.

10. Richard Hofstadter, *Social Darwinism in American Thought* (New York: George Braziller, 1959), p. 47,

11. Ibid., p. 66.

12. Andrew Carnegie, *Autobiography of Andrew Carnegie* (Boston: Houghton Mifflin, 1920), p. 206.

13. Thomas Bell, *Out of This Furnace* (Pittsburgh: University of Pittsburgh Press, 1976).

14. Roy Lubove, *Twentieth Century Pittsburgh* (New York: John Wiley & Sons, 1969), pp. 59–60.

15. *Pittsburgh Post-Gazette*, January 7, 1982, pp. 1, 17; *Pittsburgh*, November 1986, pp. 74–79.

16. The origins of the black experience in Pittsburgh are dramatically portrayed in two novels by John Edgar Wideman: *Damballah* (New York: Avon Books, 1981) and *Hiding Place* (New York: Avon Books, 1981).

17. Proposal for a consultation on "Seminaries, the Church and Social Policy: Theological Education and the Common Good," ACCS, June 4, 1986.

Chapter 5. Getting Our Priorities Straight

1. Bonganjalo Goba, "A Black South African Perspective," in Virginia Fabella and Sergio Torres, *Doing Theology in a Divided World* (Maryknoll, NY: Orbis, 1985), p. 58.

2. James Cone, "Black Theology: Its Origin, Methodology, and Relationship to Third World Theologies," in Fabella and Torres, *Doing Theology*, p. 99.

3. For example, a few years ago I had the privilege of traveling in Greece and Egypt. In both of those places I saw tremendous poverty and struggle. I was touched by what I saw. But this feeling is not yet "praxis," which would require my active involvement and commitment to the cause of those poor people I saw on my travels.

4. Pablo Richard, "Nicaragua: Basic Church Communities in a Revolutionary Situation," in Fabella and Torres, *Doing Theology*, p. 31.

5. Georges Casalis, "Methodology for a West European Theology of Liberation," in Fabella and Torres, *Doing Theology*, p. 106.

6. Richard, "Nicaragua," p. 31.

7. Mercy Amba Oduyoye, "Who Does Theology? Reflections on the Subject of Theology," in Fabella and Torres, *Doing Theology*, p. 47.

8. The Mud Flower Collective (Katie Cannon et al.), *God's Fierce Whimsy: Christian Feminism and Theological Education* (New York: The Pilgrim Press, 1985), p. 145.

9. Ibid., p. 133.

10. Basil Moore, "What Is Black Theology?" in *Black Theology: The South African Voice* (London: C. Hurst, 1973), p. 6.

11. Mud Flower, *God's Fierce Whimsy*, p. 161.

12. I have tried to deal with the realities of being both oppressed

and oppressor in *Justice in an Unjust World: Foundations for a Christian Approach to Justice* (Minneapolis: Augsburg, 1988).

13. Note, however, that to do so is often to put the student in the role of teacher, and to put the teacher in the role of listener.

14. The use of pain as an educational tool is further discussed in Karen Lebacqz, "Pain and Pedagogy: A Modest Proposal," in *Discipleship and Citizenship,* ed. Mary C. Boys (forthcoming from The Pilgrim Press).

15. Cone, "Black Theology: Its Origin," p. 102.

16. See Elisabeth Schüssler-Fiorenza, *In Memory of Her: A Feminist Theological Reconstruction of Christian Origins* (New York: Crossroad, 1984) and *Bread Not Stone: The Challenge of Feminist Biblical Interpretation* (Boston: Beacon Press, 1984).

17. Steve Biko, "Black Consciousness and the Quest for a True Humanity," in Moore, *Black Theology,* p. 45.

18. James Cone, "Black Theology and Black Liberation," in Moore, *Black Theology,* p. 50.

19. Sheila D. Collins, *A Different Heaven and Earth: A Feminist Perspective on Religion* (Valley Forge, PA: Judson Press, 1974).

20. Malcolm X, quoted by Cone in "Black Theology: Its Origin," p. 100.

21. Sabelo Ntwasa, "The Training of Black Ministers Today," in Moore, *Black Theology,* p. 145.

22. Wil Blezer van de Walle, "The Netherlands: Women Speaking Equality," in Fabella and Torres, *Doing Theology,* p. 24.

23. Cone, "Black Theology and Black Liberation," pp. 56–57.

24. Cf. Jose Miguez-Bonino, *Toward a Christian Political Ethics* (Philadelphia: Fortress Press, 1983).

25. Ada Maria Isasi-Diaz quoted in Mud Flower, *God's Fierce Whimsy,* p. 90.

26. Mud Flower, *God's Fierce Whimsy,* p. 203.

27. This woman was Caucasian but had lived in and identified with the black community for many years.

28. Cf. Rosemary Radford Ruether, *"A Feminist Perspective,"* in Fabella and Torres, *Doing Theology,* p. 65.

29. Ntwasa, "The Training of Black Ministers," p. 142.

30. Biko, "Black Consciousness," p. 40.

31. Mud Flower, *God's Fierce Whimsy,* pp. 95–96.

32. Ibid., p. 94.

33. Bruce Gilbard, "Community Priests in the New Zealand Anglican Church," *Ministerial Formation* 34 (June 1986): 8.

34. Ibid.

35. For a discussion of character in the professions, see Lebacqz,

Professional Ethics: Power and Paradox (Nashville: Abingdon Press, 1984).

36. The result, charges Joseph D. Ban in "Christological Foundations of Theological Education," *Ministerial Formation* 34 (June 1986): 16, is a supposedly Christian education that is really a "replica of civil religion." While he makes this charge of Christian schools in general, I think it might also be applied to seminaries.

37. Ibid., p. 20.

38. Mary Weir, "Theology with a Human Face," *Ministerial Formation* 33 (March 1986): 19.

39. Janet F. Fishburn and Neil Q. Hamilton, "Seminary Education Tested by Praxis," *The Christian Century*, February 1–8, 1984, pp. 108–12.

40. Ibid., p. 111.

41. Moore, "What Is Black Theology?" p. 7.

42. Mud Flower, *God's Fierce Whimsy*, p. 204.

43. Ibid., p. 158.

44. Ibid., p. 122.

45. I have provided some discussion of the ways in which structures limit professional freedom in *Professional Ethics*.

46. Professional society meetings tend to be organized so that one reads a written essay in absolute defiance of the well-known facts that the spoken and the written word are two different media.

47. Cf. van de Walle, "The Netherlands."

48. I am told that there is at least one seminary in India where the students are required to live for six months in the slums as prelude to their theological study. Such an approach seems to be consonant with the praxis ideal.

Chapter 6. Focusing on the Church's Mission

1. *Mission and Evangelism: An Ecumenical Affirmation* (Geneva: World Council of Churches, 1983).

2. Lesslie Newbigin, *The Other Side of 1984* (Geneva: World Council of Churches, 1984), and *Foolishness to the Greeks: The Gospel and Western Culture* (Grand Rapids: Eerdmans, 1986).

3. Newbigin, *Foolishness to the Greeks*, p. 94.

4. For a discussion on Peter Taylor Forsyth and his doctrine of the church, see Robert S. Paul, *Freedom with Order* (New York: United Church Press, 1987), pp. 113–23.

5. George A. Lindbeck, *The Nature of Doctrine: Religion and Theology in a Postliberal Age* (Philadelphia: Westminster Press, 1984).

6. William H. Willimon, "Making Christians in a Secular World," *The Christian Century,* October 22, 1986, pp. 914–17.

Chapter 7. Learning with the Justice-active Church

1. I intend this chapter to be theologically responsive to New Reformation ecclesiology and to basic accents of Reformed thought. A careful exploration of its thesis may shed new light on the seminary's vocational dilemma over how much to be an academy that emphasizes biblical-theological-ethical-historical-behavorial science inquiry, and how much to teach professional pastoral practice. For background on this issue, see Edward Farley, *Theologica: Fragmentation and Unity Theological Education* (Philadelphia: Fortress Press, 1983), and Charles M. Wood, *Vision and Discernment: An Orientation in Theological Study* (Atlanta: Scholars Press, 1985).
2. Cf. my paper on "Christian Ethics and the Congregation's Social Ministry," delivered to and published in the *Annual* of the 25th anniversary meeting of the Society of Christian Ethics (1984). Some of my books explore church controversy over social involvement (*Reconciliation and Conflict,* Philadelphia: Westminster Press, 1969), strategy and styles of church-based public engagement (*A Social Action Primer,* Philadelphia: Westminster Press, 1972), a whole conception of local church praxis (*Social Ministry,* Philadelphia: Westminster Press, 1982).
3. Cf. William E. Gibson, "Eco-Justice: New Perspective for a Time of Turning," in Dieter T. Hessel, ed., *For Creation's Sake* (Philadelphia: Westminster/Geneva, 1985), ch. 1.
4. See *Shalom Connections in Personal and Congregational Life* (Ellenwood, GA: Alternatives, 1986).
5. Dana W. Wilbanks and Ronald H. Stone, *Presbyterians and Peacemaking: Are We Now Called to Resistance?* (New York: Advisory Council on Church and Society, 1986), introduce an ethic of just peace and explore a moral stance of resisting the policies of the national security state. They emphasize that resistance seeks the transformation of the political order by making and standing against demonic policies that corrupt it and by political action aimed at basic change.
6. Hessel, *Social Ministry* (Philadelphia: Westminster Press, 1982).
7. Barbara Brown Zikmund, *Discovering the Church* (Philadelphia: Westminster Press, 1983), chs. 1 and 2.
8. Celia A. Hahn, *Lay Voices in an Open Church* (Washington, DC: Alban Institute, 1986), observes that churchgoers most want "to be drawn into a loving community" that offers energizing meaning as

well as support for the private sphere of relationships. "We laity are asking for a caring community and religion that gives meaning to life. We want our churchgoing to strengthen us for the struggles we encounter every day. Our yearning for connections between 'the transcendent vision and the everyday reality' seems most evident in the deeply cherished arena of family life, less clear in the enormously complex public spheres beyond."

Hahn notes that many members of the church are perplexed about drawing, and actually despair of sustaining, meaningful connections between faith, work, and politics. Her discussion pictures the church in conventional terms as a liturgical gathering and warm fellowship that inspires and sustains people for dispersed individual ministries. Missing from her purview is a New Reformation ecclesiology featuring vital church groups—today we call them base-community structures of the church—that nourish the laity and use their gifts in doing shared ministry.

9. James Gustafson, *Treasure in Earthen Vessels* (Chicago: University of Chicago Press, 1961), analyzes the personal-social functions of the community that centers on the person-event of Jesus Christ. But Gustafson puts the functional analysis in theological-ethical context, noting that the church is the historical, human community of liturgical and moral loyalty to the One who purposes to create, sustain, restrain, and redeem. In light of God's purpose, we can appreciate and develop three social functions—which are also mission purposes—of the faith community: to worship under biblical discipline, to nurture personal growth in community, and to witness faithfully in society. A congregation that does all three works to transform (a) cultural ethos, (b) interpersonal relations, and (c) institutional life, including politics.

10. Cf. James Davidson et al., "Increasing Church Involvement in Social Concerns," *Review of Religious Research* 29 (Summer 1979): 291–96.

Common functions of the whole people of God stated in *PCUSA Form of Government*, ch. 5, are to share the ministry of proclaiming the good news (see [a] below), by embodying it through life together in the church (see [b] through [e]) and through life and witness in society (see [f] through [i]). Faithful members join in:

a. proclaiming the good news;
b. taking part in the common life and worship of a particular church;
c. praying and studying scripture and faith heritage;
d. supporting the work of the Church through giving money, time and talents;

e. participating in governing the [local] church;

f. demonstrating a new quality of life within and through the church;

g. responding to God's activity in the world through service to others;

h. living responsibly in personal, family, work, political, cultural, and social relationships of life; and

i. working the world for peace, justice, freedom and human fulfillment.

11. Alasdair MacIntyre, *After Virtue: A Study in Moral Theory* (Notre Dame, IN: University of Notre Dame Press, 1984).

12. Briefs for various emphases and methods appear in papers by Rosemary Ruether, Gordon Kaufman, Langdon Gilkey, John Cobb, James Cone, and others in Theodore W. Jennings Jr., ed., *The Vocation of the Theologian* (Philadelphia: Fortress Press, 1985).

13. Joseph Hough and John Cobb, *Christian Identity and Theological Education* (Atlanta: Scholars Press, 1985), ch. 5, on "The Education of Practical Theologians," offer more pointed suggestions to grapple with the global context than to engage local need.

14. George D. Younger, *From New Creation to Urban Crisis: A History of Action Training Ministries 1962–75* (Chicago: Center for the Scientific Study of Religion, 1987), ponders the demise of urban training because of its problematic distance from integrated theological study and the seminary.

Chapter 8. Developing Eyes and Ears for Social Ministry

1. *Directory for the Service of God,* Ch. 6.05, in the *Book of Order* of the reunited Presbyterian Church (USA), 1983.

2. In addition to the classic works by these authors, J. Milton Yinger provides a good selection of such material in *Religion, Society and the Individual* (New York: Macmillan, 1957). For more recent material on some of the social functions of the church, see Robin Gill, *Prophecy and Praxis: The Social Function of the Churches* (London: Marshall, Morgan & Scott, 1981), and Gregory Baum, *Religion and Alienation* (New York: Paulist Press, 1975).

3. D.B. McPherson, *The Political Theory of Possessive Individualism: Hobbs to Locke* (Oxford: University Press, 1962); Fronz J. Hinkelammert, *The Ideological Weapons of Death* (Maryknoll, NY: Orbis, 1986); Peter Berger, Brigette Berger, and Honsfried Kellner, *The Homeless Mind* (New York: Random House, 1973); Charles Birch and John

Cobb Jr., *The Liberation of Life* (New York: Cambridge University Press, 1981); and Douglas J. Hall, *Imaging God: Dominion as Stewardship* (New York: William B. Eerdmans and Friendship Press, 1986), are sample works that explore these three motifs.

4. See Roger Hutchinson and Gibson Winter, "Towards a Method in Political Ethics," in *Perspectives on Political Ethics*, ed. Kason Srisong (Geneva: World Council of Churches, 1983).

5. The phrase is Jose Miguez-Bonino's, in *Toward a Christian Political Ethics* (Philadelphia: Fortress Press, 1983).

6. Gibson Winter has led the way in relating beliefs and values to the social sciences in social analysis in *Elements for a Social Ethic* (New York: Macmillan, 1966) and *Liberating Creation: Foundations of Religious Social Ethics* (New York: Crossroad, 1981). See also the important work of William W. Everett and T.J. Bachmeyer, *Disciplines in Transformation* (Washington, DC: University Press of America, 1979).

7. See Katherine Doob Sakenfeld, *The Meaning of Hesed in the Hebrew Bible* (Missoula, MT: Scholars Press, 1978) and *Faithfulness in Action: Loyalty in Biblical Perspective* (Philadelphia: Fortress Press, 1985).

8. The phrase, carefully worded, is John C. Bennett's, *The Radical Imperative* (Philadelphia: Westminster Press, 1975), p. 14.

9. See, for example, James W. Douglass, *Lightning East to West* (New York: Crossroad, 1983).

10. See especially *Social Ministry* (Philadelphia: Westminster Press, 1982).

11. An example of attending to the social dimension in preaching is *Preaching as a Social Act*, ed. Art Van Seters (Nashville: Abingdon Press, 1988).

Chapter 9. Tradition and Change: Curricular Trends in the Recent History of Theological Education

1. I am also grateful for the insights of the institutions' deans and Consultation participants who clarified the documents and sources in ways no nonliving thing can.

2. "A Theological Curriculum for the 1970s," *Theological Education*, Spring 1968.

3. The other proposed centers were classified by the kind of ministry they represented and were Ministry through institutions, Ministry through political process, Crisis Ministry, and Ministry through the arts.

4. *Interdenominational Theological Center 1986–87 Catalogue*, vol. xxvi, pp. 54–55.

5. *Wesley Theological Seminary, 1985–86 Catalogue*, pp. 36–37.

6. *Eastern Baptist Theological Seminary, 1983–85 Catalogue*, p. 45.

7. *Virginia Theological Seminary Catalogue, 1986–87*, p. 9.

8. *Eastern Baptist Theological Seminary, 1983–85 Catalogue*, pp. 10–13.

9. "Report of the Self-Study," Pittsburgh Theological Seminary, February 15, 1970.

10. "Report of the Curriculum Revision Task Force, 1983–85 Interdenominational Theological Center." Revised edition, May 8, 1985, p. 32.

11. James M. Gustafson. "Christian Ethics," in *Religion*, ed. Paul Ramsey (Englewood Cliffs, NJ: Prentice-Hall, 1965), pp. 287–92.